RUN TO THE ROAR

RUN TO THE ROAR

by Tammy Bakker
with Cliff Dudley

New Leaf Press
P.O. BOX 1045. HARRISON. ARK. 72601

Photo Credits:
Front Cover — Phil Egert
Back Cover — Eddie Holder

First printing, May 1980
Second printing, June 1980
Third printing, April 1982

Springfield, Mo. 65802

"Through the typesetting of this book, I am on my way to complete victory over the fears that have tormented me most of my life!"

--Twyla Menzies

Library of Congress Catalog Card Number: 80-80656

International Standard Book Number: 0-89221-073-7

DEDICATION

I dedicate this book to my precious husband, Jim Bakker, who has loved me in spite of my fears and has helped me RUN TO THE ROAR!

CONTENTS

FOREWORD

A number of years ago, while I was visiting Mexico City, a since-deceased friend of mine, Fito Best Maugard, showed me the manuscript of an exhaustive book of research he had just completed. Fito was a great painter and a prime mover of that school of art which came to be known as the Mexican Renaissance, and which spawned such figures as Orozco, Rivera, and others.

As a student, Fito had made hundreds of sketches of temple friezes, not only in Mexico but in Italy and Greece as well, and in the process had been startled to discover that there were in all but twelve basic symbols used over and over again. His studies led him on to recognize these same symbols in subsequent and more highly sophisticated art forms, and he was able to postulate that each one represented a human emotion which the artist could no more avoid using than could a finger the scale.

The most intriguing of the twelve to me was the Z, to which Fito assigned a dual significance: fear and fury. In response to my somewhat skeptical reaction he asked me if I had ever seen lightning portrayed with the Z-form.

"Often," I replied.

"But have you ever seen real lightning that looked like a Z?"

"No," I confessed.

"Of course not," he smiled. "Real lightning has the shape of a tree with the branches stretching across the heavens. The Z represents man's age-old fear of lightning!"

"All right," I conceded, "but where does the fury come in?"

"Let's suppose," he continued, "that you're talking on the telephone and doodling idly with a pencil in your free hand, when something is said by the person on the other end of the line of such a nature as to throw you into a perfect frenzy of rage. With the pencil you are likely to slash out a series of continuous Z's violent enough to rip the paper to shreds and break the pencil as well; but it won't be U's you'll be making, or spirals or circles—it will be Z's and only Z's."

I mean to suggest by this illustration that as fear and unbridled fury has a common outlet, a common expression in man's nature, we are dealing with something, when we speak of fear, of so ominous a character that we can easily see why, as Tammy Bakker points out, the fearful are consigned to the lake of fire along with murderers, whoremongers, and other lapidicolous species.

Fear is far from the harmless vice many suppose it to be. Indeed, there are no harmless vices, and Tammy aptly indentifies fear at its best as an arrogant vote of no-confidence in God's ability or inclination to protect His own.

This book is a frank, thoughtful, and self-revealing investigation of the many forms of fear to which we are all subject, but our gaze is continually directed back through time to a cross on a hill where the greatest struggle in history was worked out in mute agony, and victory won of such enormity that the power of fear or any other sin to hold mankind in thralldom was forever after shattered. All that remains, we are reminded, is for the faithful to lay claim to that victory.

Finally, through the pages of this endearing book there emerges the portrait of a gallant Christian lady whom, pound for pound I should judge, Satan would least cherish meeting on a dark night!

From a loving Christian brother,

Efrem Zimbalist Jr.

Chapter 1

A PRIDE OF LIONS

PTL—Multi-Million Dollar Business

PTL To Be Investigated By FCC

PTL Host's 'Dream Home' For Sale; He Has Another

PTL Must Tell What It Spends

These and many other suggestive headlines have appeared in newspapers across America. At times I didn't think I could take the pressure. Fear gripped my heart!

For many months PTL, but especially Jim and I, have been really harassed by the media, mainly the newspapers. The newspapers have written some really terrible stories about PTL. They have even written lies, just total lies about us.

There were times when we'd spot the reporters with sunglasses on sitting out in front of our house in old beat-up cars, hoping we wouldn't recognize them. We would find them almost everywhere we went. The world just doesn't understand the things of the Lord, and because of these articles there were many people who started to think that we were out for nothing but money and who thought that we were just no good.

The newspaper had a picture of our house on the front page. I was afraid people were going to come and destroy it because not only was our house on the front page but also our address. Even the boat we bought was on the front page, where it was located, how much we paid for it. Everything that we had seemed to end up on the front page of the local newspaper.

It looked like they literally were trying to destroy PTL. Then because of their stories the Federal Communications Commission came in on us. People thought, "Boy, if the FCC is coming in on PTL, there surely has to be something wrong because those charges just don't come in for no reason."

This, of course, put fear in us, terrible fear. We had somebody stay with us and guard the house all the time. We even had double locks put on our doors.

Then threats started coming. Jim couldn't handle these threats against the children and me. We had threats to bomb our house, threats to bomb our studio, and threats to kidnap our children. What were we supposed to do? Then a call came, "If your two children aren't out of town by six o'clock tonight, they are going to end up missing." Fear almost overtook us. It was the kind of fear where you were afraid to lay your head down on the pillow at night. You didn't know what reading the newspaper had incited in somebody's heart that didn't love the Lord. It was terrible, terrible.

One night late in the evening when we got home, Jim turned to me and said, "Tammy, you are going to Florida tomorrow!" He just shocked me with that statement.

I cried and said, "Why, Honey, why?"

His only reply was, "Tammy, the less you know, the better off you will be. Honey, just trust me."

I started crying and sobbing. "Honey, you gotta tell me what's wrong! You gotta. Jim, you have never kept anything from me; why are you doing it now? Jim, Jim, say something!" Jim had kept a lot of the threats pretty much away from me, although I knew of the bombing threats. That was nothing new; for years we had had those. But now I knew something serious had happened for Jim to send me away and not tell me why.

Slowly Jim turned to me and whispered, "Honey, don't tell Tammy Sue or say anything to Jamie, but their lives have been threatened." All of a sudden, Jim burst out sobbing and threw his arms around me and said, "I love you so much, and I'm going to send you away. I don't know how long you are going to have to be gone. Oh God, help us. Please God, do something!"

I questioned God and asked, "How can You let this happen?"

"Jim," I said, "I want to stay here with you. You need me Jim. You need me. Will you be O.K.?" I was afraid that they were going to come back and kill him.

Jim said, "Tammy, I'll be all right. I have people around me, but you and the children have to leave, and now!"

So we were sent away from our own home. I didn't know what to pack. I didn't know how long I was going to be gone, so I didn't even know how many suitcases to take. I was almost out of my mind with fear. I didn't even know where we were going. We were just given an address. I had never met the people and didn't have any idea who they were.

I called my girlfriend, Beverly Wright, and she

quit work to come and go with me. She was a dear friend from CBN days. We got up early in the morning, before it was hardly light, and got into our car and slowly drove away. They guarded us until we got out of town for fear that somebody was going to see us leave.

There we were—two women and three kids—not even knowing to whom we were going or what was going to happen. One of the loneliest feelings that I've ever had in my life was pulling out of the driveway and looking back seeing Jim standing there all alone. We were on our way. The miles that passed seemed like hours upon hours and days upon days. The fear that gripped my heart was almost choking me; not knowing the people to whose house we were going or anything about them was as bad as anything I had ever felt. Everything seemed to be shrouded in mystery. Of course, I understood that it was absolutely necessary that no one would know where we were going or how we could be reached. It was for our own security and safety. I knew now that our very lives were at stake!

After what seemed like a week, and it really was only a couple of days, we arrived at the designated home in Florida.

As the car pulled into the driveway, I sat there frozen with fear. I have always had such a fear of meeting people (believe it or not), and now what was going to happen? Finally I got the courage to open the car door, and we slowly got out and walked toward the house. Five refugees in exile until God would deliver us.

I slowly lifted my hand to ring the bell. Jamie and Tammy Sue stood beside me totally bewildered. I heard the bell ring, and my mind took off. "Oh, Jesus, what are they like? Will they understand? Do they like children? Will the kids break something?" On and on my mind raced.

The door suddenly opened and there they stood. The pastor, full of smiles, said, "Tammy, praise the Lord, you have arrived safely. We sure do love you. Please, all of you, come in."

Instantly I began to feel at peace in their home. I quickly found out that we had met this pastor's wife's sister many, many months prior to this when we were vacationing in Florida, and this is how Jim had gotten in touch with them. It was obvious, as we entered the home, that they could see on my face that I was in absolute agony and overcome with grief and fear. He must have looked at my children, that little girl and that little boy, and saw their bewilderment and fear.

The pastor's wife had baked some cookies, so we sat down at the table and began to give a little sigh of relief. Yet that gnawing sensation was in the back of my mind. "How many days will I sit at this table? Will I ever see Jim alive again? What is going to happen to PTL? What is this going to do to the emotions of the children?" Once again the tears began to flow.

As I was pondering all of these things in my heart, the pastor looked me square in the eye and said, *"Tammy, I have a story that God wants me to share with you. I feel that I must do it, and now. Tammy, I was a missionary in Africa, and I want to tell you something that I learned while I was there. It is a simple but profound story. It is a story about the lions. As a matter of fact, about a pride of lions. Pride, by the way, means a group or herd of lions.*

"This particular story is about the old king. You see, a lion can only be the king as long as he is strong enough to hold his position. There is always someone

fighting and trying to take over the kingship. Usually by the time the old king is kicked out, he doesn't have any teeth and only a few claws. His hair is all matted; he has arthritis in the joints, and he no longer can fight to keep his position. So a younger lion becomes the new king.

"But it is interesting, Tammy; you see, they don't throw him out completely. He still has his place in the pride. However, now his sole job in the pride is to roar when they go on their hunts. When the lions go hunting, the great big old mean-looking ferocious lion, with no teeth and no claws, stands to one side. And over to the other side, hidden in the bushes and thickets, are all the young hunter lions.

"When all of a sudden the antelope pops out of the bushes, the great big old lion, the former king, looks at it and begins to roar. That old lion's roar scares that little animal so bad that it runs the other way . . . right into the waiting jaws of the hunter lions who tear him to pieces and destroy him. If that poor little prey had only run toward the roar, there wouldn't have been a thing that could hurt him. The old lion was too old and weak. All he had left was his roar.

"The Bible says the devil is going around as a roaring lion seeking whom he may devour. But, praise God, he has already been defeated. All he has left is a scary roar; Jesus took care of that! He's just a mean, hateful old devil that has been defeated at the Cross of Calvary. He can't do anything to us.

"The big mistake we make as Christians is that we run away from him. As we run away from him, we run right into all the imps of hell who torment us and fill us with fear and defeat. Many people are destroyed by fear and torment by these imps because they do *not run toward their fears.*

"*The Bible says that David, when he went up to kill the giant, ran toward him. He ran toward his fear. Now, you know that David (they say he wasn't very big), with only five pebbles from a brook, must have been afraid of that old giant. But he ran toward that giant, flung that stone, and the God that we serve caused that giant to fall down on the ground dead!! Tammy, giants in our lives can be destroyed if we as David run toward those giants. Run towards their roar. Run towards their bigness. Run towards whatever it is, and we are going to see it defeated in the name of Jesus.*"

As he finished, a hush came over the kitchen. We sat there in silence. The Holy Spirit was ministering truth to me. Even the children were awed and hushed. I sat there stunned, for I realized that the better part of my life I was like that poor little antelope. I would hop out of the bushes in the happiness of the Lord, and all of a sudden I would hear the roar, and I would run into the imps of hell and be terrified, sometimes for months, and almost be devoured.

Tears came streaming down my cheeks as the impact of his story hit me. It surged into my mind and into my heart, and then something within me snapped, and I saw the truth of the Word of God. I was set free instantly. I was set free. I was totally free.

That moment I got up and called Jim and told him the story. Over and over again I said to him on the telephone, "Jim, Honey, I have been set free. Really, Honey, I have been set free. I am free of the bondage of fear. I believe now I will be able to run to the roar; I will be able to run toward Satan covered with the blood of Jesus, because He hasn't given me the spirit of fear, but of power, love, and a sound mind. Jim,

Honey, I'm free. I'm free!"

At the time I don't think I even realized the full impact of what was happening to me. However, I knew beyond a shadow of a doubt that a new surge of faith had come into me, into my heart.

I didn't realize that I had been set free to fly, but I knew that faith had come into my heart, and I shared that faith with Jim. That story helped him so much; it was absolutely unbelievable the faith that Jim had in facing the threats, the crises at home, and even the FCC hearings. Right away my new faith began to help Jim's also.

It totally, instantaneously, set me free. I did not have another fear at that moment. We stayed in Florida for about three weeks. God gave us a motel with an indoor swimming pool, and we had the times of our lives. The kids swam every day and there was even a shopping center close by where I could do some shopping.

Then Jim and Tom, Bev's husband, called and said, "We're flying down to take you home." We had a grand vacation with our husbands for two or three days. God turned what the devil had meant for bad to be one of the greatest victories in my life. I asked Jim how he knew it was time for us to go home.

"Things have quieted down totally at home," he said, "and your being sent away was on the front page of the paper. The city heard about it, and they were so appalled by something like that, that they had great sympathy."

This chapter, now that I have finished it, makes faith seem oh so simple. But when I look back over the years, boy, whew, it has really been scary! Fear really all started . . . when . . .

Chapter 2

FEARS OF CHILDREN

The boogie man will get you if you don't watch out!

God won't love you if you do that!

Bad children burn in hell!

If you don't go to Sunday school, Jesus won't love you anymore!

The darkness seemed to overtake me! I felt a presence in the room. "What is it?" I thought. I opened my eyes, but I could hardly see my hand in front of my face. Then I heard the creak of the stairs. Someone was on the stair-steps. The sound came closer and closer. Who is it? What is it? "Someone help me. Please, someone help me!" I thought. I am going to be murdered.

Oh, I know Jesus has come, and I've been left. Why didn't I mind mama better? Jesus, I really love you. I really do!

"Tammy, Tammy, breakfast is ready. Why, didn't you come the first time I called?"

19

"Oh, mama; oh, mama!" I was so thankful that I had only had a nightmare, but during the day I still worried about being left behind when Jesus came.

Fear in the life of a child often starts out as a "fun thing," like riding on the rides at the fair or being told a scary fairy tale. Jamie Charles, my son, just loves to hear a scary story. We'll come to that scary part, and although he's heard it fifteen times, his little face just tenses up, he gets scared, and he'll say, "Now, tell it again."

Look at all the fairy tales we read our children. Most of them are terrible. Here are some examples:

Hansel and Gretel. The story of two children abandoned by their father in the forest to starve to death. They are captured by the witch and end up shoving her in the oven to bake to death.

Little Red Riding Hood. Grandmother is eaten by a big bad wolf.

Three Little Pigs. Pigs are eaten by the wolf, and the wolf boils at the bottom of the fireplace.

Snowwhite. Eats a poisoned apple given to her by the bad witch.

Jack and the Bean Stalk. The giant at the top of the clouds (a God image) eats people for a pastime. Jack is almost one of them. But he cuts the stalk down, and the giant falls to his death.

Alice in Wonderland. The queen is obsessed with cutting off everyone's heads.

The list could go on and on, but I think you see my point. Most of us have never thought that these stories could be harmful to a child.

Today an even greater menace to the minds of children is television. Saturday morning cartoons are almost 100 percent Godless and giving glory and place to false gods, idols, and demons. Children like to be afraid. That is why they produce movies for the kids like *The Frankenstein Monster*. People go by the thousands to be scared. But the tragedy is that there is a point where fear isn't fun anymore. Playing with it can be very dangerous to you, and there is a point where you can go too far.

When I was little, I used to go over to my girlfriend's house to play. She had a little playhouse, and all of us kids would get in that little house, and we'd tell ghost stories and haunted-house stories. We would get so scared that we actually couldn't get out and go home. Her mother would have to come and open the door and take us kids home because we would be so frightened. For some strange reason we enjoyed that fear. We'd go back to the playhouse and tell the stories again and again and again, scaring ourselves senseless, but we had fun doing it.

I don't really remember the day when fun started to go into fear that would really damage my life—from fantasy to reality. My aunt and uncle lived out in the country, and we'd look out over the vast areas with hardly any homes and see lights all over and say, "What's that? What's that, Grandma and Grandpa? What's that Aunt Tutie?"

And they would say, "Those are swamp kitties on the loose tonight." We'd have the biggest imaginations of what a swamp kitty was, and they kept getting bigger and bigger. So entered the fear of the nights and darkness.

I remember one night that we stayed out in a tent, way out in the back yard. We scared ourselves so bad by telling ourselves stories in the middle of the night that my parents had to come and get us, yelling and screaming, and put us to bed inside.

I believe that most fears come from our parents when they start putting fear in us through punishment. They start saying, "If you don't behave, I'm going to spank you!" At a very young age as a child I had a fear of not pleasing my parents or God. I believe that's part of the fear that stays with you into adulthood—the fear that you're not going to please your parents.

When you get out in the world, you're then afraid you're not going to please others. You love them so much you want to please them. You're afraid of rejection, so you want to please them. There's a big difference there between the real love and the fear. We should want to please our parents because we love them so much. Most of us, I think, that were raised in my day and age obeyed our parents because we were so frightened by what they would do to us if we didn't.

Both parents and the church kept us under a bondage of the fear of punishment.

Sometimes as a child it was really strange; I would pray, but I never thought God would answer my prayers. I was afraid I wasn't good enough for Him to answer. As a very small child I accepted Jesus as my Saviour. I received the baptism of the Holy Spirit when I was ten years old, and did that make a big difference in my life! Then I knew God as never before. I mean, I knew if I prayed and asked God to take care of me, that He would.

Satan wants to break our trust in God, and he will use any opportunity he can to create fear within us.

The first time I rode on an airplane was right after Jim and I were married. I wasn't afraid—not in the least. I boarded the airplane in International Falls, Minnesota, and flew to Minneapolis. So my first airplane ride in the whole world was from International Falls to Minneapolis. I had never heard of any airplanes crashing or mechanical trouble, so I was at peace. I had not even seen an airplane up close before, so I didn't know that there was even the slightest reason to be afraid of airplanes. I thought everybody always made it on an airplane.

Then I saw my first airplane crash. And fear came! If you don't know that something can happen, you don't fear it. But when I saw that airplane crash, then that fear came crashing in. We were at the airport waiting for the arrival of Jim's mother. The airport was small, so we could watch her airplane arrive.

The weather was terrible; it was snowing so hard that you could hardly see anything in front of you. The planes were running late, and we heard that they had closed the airport to all planes except the one we were waiting for.

The plane circled the airport for about two hours, but finally its fuel was so low that it had to land. Long before we could see the plane, we heard it make its approach. All of a sudden the plane seemed to fall out of the sky. Everyone who was waiting started screaming, "The plane has crashed! The plane has crashed!" At that, I also started screaming.

The plane had hit a snowplow that was near the runway. Soon we saw the people start coming out of the plane on chutes. There were servicemen that were helping the people get out. Some of the people were being dragged out with blood all over them. Everyone seemed to be screaming and crying, more from hysteria than pain.

But that moment took its toll on my life. For Satan put a fear in my heart that would haunt me for years to come. It would hinder my ministry and mobility for the Lord's work. Jim's mom was all right, and everyone seemed O.K. but me. Little did I know then the terrible grip that Satan had on my life. I felt right then and there that never again would I get on an airplane.

We as parents need to be extremely careful how we deal with fear in the lives of our children. And how important it is that when they do experience a trauma in their lives, that we reassure them of God's protection, God's love, and God's care and concern.

I was with my parents; we were riding down this rural road in a Model A Ford. I was scarcely three years old, and it's interesting even as I tell this story how it seems as though it was only moments ago. I'd never been afraid of cars—never had given a thought that there was anything to fear about being in a car—when all of a sudden the car went off the road, and we slammed into a ditch.

Instantly there was panic. The car was just ready to flip, and I picked up quickly the fear that was in the voice of my father and my mother. I was so terrified that I started screaming uncontrollably, and no one seemed to be concerned about comforting me. I could hear the men who obviously had come from the nearby homes, saying, "Watch it; watch it. Don't let the children get pinned in the car." And they kept talking, "Hurry up before the car falls on one of them."

That impression stuck with me for many years to come. Ever since that day I have been terrified of going too fast in a car for fear that a blowout or something will happen. And I look back, and again I realize the subtlety of Satan as he places fear in our lives.

My experiences in school were always very happy. I loved going to school. It was such an excitement in my life to start the process of learning, and I could hardly wait to get dressed and be on my way to school. Till one day in second grade the teacher accused me of plugging up the drains with paper towels. And I hadn't done it! I tried to explain to her that someone else surely must have done it, but I stood accused. Nothing that I could say would change her mind.

Again, the fear of teachers and those in authority over me took its toll. And I'm sure that that teacher, several days later, would not even remember scolding me like she did. But I was such a sensitive child that it did me great harm. I think before we accuse little children of doing things, we should make very sure how we talk to them and whether or not they have indeed done something.

From that moment on it seemed like everything that happened in the classroom, every jar of paint that was broken, anything that was missing, or if a water cooler would clog or a light bulb would go out, I was always afraid that somehow I was going to get blamed for it, and I couldn't prove that I hadn't done it. That has always been a terrible fear with me that I am going to be blamed for something that I can't prove that I didn't do.

Also, in Minnesota we had very long bridges that crossed the lakes. Of course, you know, Minnesota is called the land of 10,000 lakes. Every once in awhile, when the snow would melt and the spring rains would come, there would be flooding. Oftentimes it would not be unusual to have a foot of water running right over the bridge. I'd look out over this vast amount of water, and I would imagine the car being swept off the bridge, and I would lie down between the seats screaming—sobbing because I was afraid that we were going to go into the water and drown.

It is interesting how some children seem to pick

up torment and fear out of almost every situation while other children seem to let nothing bother them.

Much of the fear that children have, I believe, is conditioned by the attitude that a family develops. If the family develops a constant confident attitude and pays little attention to the crises as they come, I believe the children will learn to respond in the same way.

For example, how do parents react when a little child falls. If they merely pick it up and comfort it and say little or nothing, I do not believe the child will have a great fear of falling. But if the mother or father runs to that baby and says, "Oh, poor baby. Have you been hurt?" and grabs her and checks the bottom to see if there's a bruise or a scratch and says, "Oh, mommy's baby," and carries on and on, then that child is going to develop a fear.

Jim and I have never done that in our family. My daughter is hardly afraid of anything, and her attitude is, oh, get up and try it again—even if she has a nose bleed or whatever. We don't make a big deal of it; we just say, "Come on now, Tammy, get up. Come on; try it again."

The fear that we as parents project, I believe, is the fear that the children are going to have. If the mother is screaming, the children will scream, and they will get into the sobbing, panic act. But if the mother simply says, "Oh, come on; forget it. You're not hurt," the child thinks in his mind, "Well, there's nothing really wrong," and he'll get up and go on.

Children, even at the cradle age, sense fear. For example, if a child falls out of a high chair, it will depend on the reaction of the parent whether or not the child will be afraid of the high chair. Many fears are ingrained in us when we are tiny, tiny, tiny.

Jamie's afraid of pets right now because he has never had a pet that he could relate to. Once a dog jumped all over him and knocked him down, and so now he's afraid of all pets just because of the one that knocked him down.

I know that if I had a dog around for two weeks and even if the dog knocked him down, if we were calm about it, and said, "Ah, come on; you're going to be O.K." then Jamie's fear would go away. Parents, remember; fear instills fear. Your panic instills fear in somebody else.

My mother and dad divorced when I was three years old, and that put a great fear in me. All my life I'd feared that the same thing would happen again and that I would be without a dad or a mother and be left alone like a lot of kids that I knew. I always hated to hear mother and daddy disagree because I was afraid that that was going to happen again.

So every time that mother and daddy fought, I'd run upstairs, iie down on the bed, and I'd just sob and cry. I don't know how many days of my life I spent crying because mother and daddy were having an argument, and I was so afraid—not because they had had an argument, but I was afraid that mother was going to leave dad or dad was going to ieave mother, and then where would we kids go?

One time, Jim and I were walking through a very narrow mountain passage at Rock City. It was so narrow that you could hardly walk through it. People got around me in the pass and all of a sudden I couldn't stand the closeness, and I started crying. I turned around and started running back the other way, forgetting that Tammy Sue was following me. I thought I was smothering; I couldn't stand it!

All of a sudden Tammy Sue began to sob and cry

and was shrieking. I looked around and said, "What's the matter with you?" not realizing that I had put this torturous fear into that little girl's heart. In turning around, running, and screaming myself, I had put that fear into my child. Then I realized what I had done. I ran up to her and hugged her. "Tammy Sue, I'm so sorry I scared you," I said.

We kneeled down, and I prayed that Jesus would help us both. After praying, we got up, and I took Tammy's hand and together we walked through the mountain passage.

Tammy Sue could have had that fear the rest of her life if I hadn't seen what my actions were doing to her.

Chapter 3

FEARS IN TEEN YEARS

It is so often said, "It is a shame to waste youth on the young." The teen years seem to be the years that leave such a great and lasting impression. One day you're a little child, and the next you're putting on the airs of a full-grown adult.

The emotions and feelings of the teen are power-packed. If these are not channeled properly by the parents and the church, total disaster can be the end result.

So often I believe parents are so frustrated with the teen's behavior, they simply give up. In the Scripture we read the story of how the Holy Spirit came to Mary who was only about fourteen years old and made the announcement that would change the course of all history.

Mary: the mother of Jesus, a little girl really, with child from the Holy Ghost, never having known a man but who knows only too well what her fate can be when her condition is exposed to the world.

She had already made the escape to see Elizabeth, and that was horrible. All alone in the dark; never knowing what she would run into in those renegade-infested hills. The wild animals weren't half as hard to face as these horrible ugly men. That was bad, but now she had to go home.

There is no way to conceal her pregnancy. There is no way to prove her innocence. Will they stone her? Will Joseph deny her? She loves him so much, but what can he think? How can he believe her story; it's crazy even to her, so how can her mom or her friends or her relatives or the townspeople or the elders or anyone who was not there to experience it believe a word of it? She herself wouldn't really believe her best friend if she came up with that kind of tale.

"Oh, God, I am trapped! I'm glad, but I'm scared. I know it's of You, but who will believe it? I know I have to go home, but how? I feel so cumbersome, Lord; I feel so naked—everyone can see. I can't explain first. I have to walk in like this and say, 'Please hear me.' But what if they won't? I love my mom so much, but how will she be able to understand? It seems so impossible. Will she believe in me? Uncle is such a letter-of-the-law man; will he listen? Oh, God, I cannot see the way, but I know I must go. Hold my hand, Lord. Hold my hand; and oh, God, thank You for choosing me!"

Can you imagine what Mary's parents would do today if their fourteen-year-old would come home and say, "I'm expecting, but by the Spirit of God!"

Mary, today, most likely would have been forced to have an abortion.

Or what about the story of Ruth in the Bible?

"Whither thou goest, I will go," Ruth had told Naomi, her mother-in-law.

Later, Naomi gave Ruth a scary command: "Behold, he (Boaz) winnoweth barley tonight in the threshing floor. . . . And it shall be, when he lieth down, that thou shalt mark the place where he shall lie, and thou shalt go in and uncover his feet, and lay thee down; and he will tell thee what thou shalt do.''

"And she said unto her, 'All that thou sayest unto me I will do.' ''

Obedient! Ruth was obedient to what Naomi, what the Holy Spirit, had commanded. She made no excuses, put nothing in the way of her duty.

Ruth's thoughts that night, though, must have run rampant. Her heart pounding actively in her chest, her lips trembled her reply. Her hands shaking, she gathered herself together and left the dwelling place of Naomi.

What would the townspeople say? "The slut! The HARLOT.''

Taking herself to lay with Boaz! She was setting herself up for rape. "I do not know this man. He is kind . . . but he is a man. What will he think of me? Will he know I am obedient and faithful? Or will he abuse me? Dear Lord, protect me! I am afraid. Will he hurt me? Oh, God, I fear even for my life.''

Ruth trusted God. She had not left the presence of the Holy Spirit. She was human. Human doubting and temptation do not mean one leaves the presence of God.

She was obedient to her commission from God. Her commitment to Naomi, to the Holy Spirit, had been, "Whither thou goest, I will go; And where thou lodgest, I will lodge; thy people shall be my people, and thy God my God: Where thou diest, will I die, and there will I be buried.''

Ruth was young, but she knew enough to place herself in God's hand. She knew that God was kind and wouldn't lead her into something that would hurt her.

Ruth lay by Boaz, and at midnight he awakened and noticed her lying there beside him. He was pleased that she had chosen him rather than a younger man.

Boaz had great respect for Ruth and did not touch her. Soon he sought her nearest of kin in order to gain the right to marry her. And they soon were.

Even the faithfulness of Ruth in the humble task of gleaning was used in God's purpose to bring Ruth and Boaz together. The result was to bring to the world the child Obed and eventually David and then through his blood-line the Messiah, Jesus Christ.

Today, many in the church think by making the teens fear God (and I don't mean reverence), they can keep the youth in the church. How very wrong they are. It will drive the teen away faster than anything else. Naomi must have really taught Ruth how faithful God is, or Ruth would never have trusted God enough to lead her through any circumstance that came along.

Another thing that most of the churches have always preached is that God is a God with a whip in His hand, and if you didn't ask Jesus to come into your heart every day, if you weren't always perfect, that you'd go to hell any minute. You were to be in prayer all day long.

I lived in terrible fear of that when I was a youngster. I thought I didn't dare do anything wrong because if I did, God would punish me and not take me to heaven. Anything I did wrong, immediately I asked Jesus to forgive me, and I lived in constant fear of going to hell. In fact, I lived in fear of not going in the rapture until just a few years ago.

One day Uncle Henry was gone, and I was co-hosting the PTL Club with Jim. When Jim got into heavy conversation with the guest, I found my mind wandering, because I wasn't part of the conversation.

(That isn't very nice, but it is the truth.) For a moment I was somewhere else thinking about shopping, when one of our guests got up to sing. He began singing the song "Nothing Between My Soul and the Saviour."

I wasn't thinking about God. I did not have my mind on God. I didn't even really have my mind on the program. When all of a sudden I saw a big round shaft of light. It was like it was a big culvert, and it went from my heart clear to the throne of God. I wasn't even thinking about God, and this vision hit me, right there on TV.

There wasn't one thing between my heart and Jesus.

I just burst out sobbing. I sobbed and sobbed and sobbed because I was so relieved that there I was not even thinking of Jesus or anything to do with God, and yet God said, "If I were to come right now, you would go to heaven."

That was a very powerful lesson that I learned. We don't have to be perfect to go to Him, and so we don't have to fear God. God is a God of love. He is a God of mercy, and He isn't a God to be feared. He's a God of love, and when we serve Him, it must be because we love Him, not because of fear. It should be the same with our parents. We *love* them, and that's the reason we should obey them.

Our God loves and protects us. When girls get a little older, they hear what some men and boys do to girls. Fear comes—of downtown, rapes going on, pick pockets, and of men hurting girls. Your mother, by this time, is telling you to be very careful. You know that you don't want anybody to pick you up. You never take a ride with strangers. If you see any strange men following you, you ought to tell somebody immediately.

I think that is another basic fear that comes from our mothers. It can really be disturbing to marriages, too, because it gets you off on the wrong foot as far as men are concerned, and it plants seeds in your mind that all men are bad and dangerous.

Sometimes I would think what bad things could be up there in my bedroom in the dark. I would imagine a man could get in the house, crawling through a window, and he could be up there waiting. So what's the first thing a girl does when she goes into her apartment? There might be a man under the bed or hiding somewhere. I can remember definitely looking under all the beds and everything else before I'd even go to sleep for fear there was certainly a man in the room somewhere.

I really worried about it. My heart would pound, and I couldn't go up the stairs without one of the kids or without a light on first. I still have somewhat of a fear today about things like that. I mean very, very real fears.

I had a lot of fears in my teen years. I was afraid that I wouldn't be accepted by the kids in school because our family was poor. The school we went to had more wealthy kids in it that dressed better than I did and had nicer clothes. Me, I would take the same black skirt and just change blouses for days and days at a time because we couldn't afford a lot of clothes.

I was always afraid of not being accepted by the kids because I was a person who loved the Lord. I was also afraid I wouldn't have any dates and the boys wouldn't like me. Then when I started dating, my mother put the fear in my heart that all boys are basically very sexually minded and you had better be careful (I think everybody's mother is like that.)

There was the fear of not getting home on time.

My mother used to say it's as easy to be five minutes early as it is to be five minutes late.

There would really be times when I did suffer the rejection, and that made the fear go deeper. I once heard a boy say, "I'd really like to take Tammy out, but she doesn't go to the movies or to dances. She doesn't go anywhere. Where could I take her? Where do you take a Christian girl?"

When I heard that, I thought, "Oh, I'll never get a date. I'll never be able to get a date because there are no Christians. I'm the only Christian." Because of that, I dated an unsaved boy for a long time.

It really bothered me because I knew I was going against what God said, but because I was so fearful that I wouldn't have a boyfriend, I compromised. I started working at getting them saved, but it never worked.

However, God took care of me during that relationship and courtship. It never developed into love even though I went with him for about two years. It could have, but I wouldn't allow it to because he wasn't a Christian. But I feared the whole time. I feared what God was thinking of me because I was going with an unsaved boy.

Yet I was the type of girl who wanted to date like everyone else and have someone to go to ball games and plays with at school. The guys that were Christians just didn't seem to do anything, and I didn't think they were worth dating.

During the years that I was a teen, I attended a church that was very steeped in cultural-type Christianity. By that I mean it seemed as though we were raised in such a strict environment of do's and don'ts that somewhere, somehow, it was very difficult to maintain a good, sound relationship with Jesus.

It seemed as though holiness was a list of what you could or could not do, not what your relationship was to Jesus Christ. For example, your hair had to be worn in a certain way. Your blouses all had to have long sleeves. There was no mixed bathing. Your skirts and dresses had to be a certain length. Earrings, lipstick, powder, fingernail polish, rings, jewelry—these were all forbidden.

I remember when I met some girls who were wearing a little make-up, and we were taught that any girl who wore make-up was not a Christian. However, when I got to know some of these girls, I realized that their Christian walk was even better than mine. So this again put a constant fear and anguish in me.

I really never started stepping out of that mold until long after I was married. Jim of course was filled with the same fear because he was raised the same way I was. And then we were afraid that if we didn't dress quite right or I didn't wear my hair right or if I did or did not do this, that the pastors wouldn't accept us, and our time in the evangelistic field would be cut short.

I'll never forget the time that I first asked Jim for a wig. I swear he almost lost his mind.

And he turned to me in anguish, and he said, "Oh, Tammy, what makes you think of wearing those sinful things? Of course, you can't have a wig."

He was worried sick that I was using, by this time, a little eye makeup or that I would wear beads. It seemed like everything that I did brought fear into Jim, and then it backlashed in me and brought fear into my heart.

When we got into television, I stepped somewhat out of my mold, and I began to realize that there were many people out there in the world, and I could minister, perhaps to many of them, by not being so bland; for I began to realize that Christianity is something that people want to see in our actions. And because we wear our hair a certain way or we do or do not wear make-up does not make us spiritual.

Many people were looking at us who were rather plain and were seeing the fighting and the backbiting, and we were hearing them say, "Well, if that's Christianity, I don't want any part of it."

I wanted to change that. I wanted to minister to those who did not know Jesus. So I decided I was going to step out and be me. If you would like the full blast of what's happened to me, read my book *I Gotta Be Me*.

But I decided that I was going to be the real me that I was inside, and I was going to quit this facade and this hypocrisy, and that's when I first started wearing lipstick, and I started dressing more stylish and more fashionable. And I knew on television I would appeal to some, and I also realized there would be those that I would not appeal to. But I really, for the first time in my life, decided I've got to do what I feel God wants me to do.

I actually came to the point where I said, "I don't care what they think of me. They can turn the TV off. But as long as I'm not doing something that I feel that God is displeased with, I'm going to do it."

It took me that many years to come to the realization that God cares about the condition of our *heart*. For the scripture even tells us that man looks on the outward appearance, but God looks upon the heart. God is far more concerned about what's going on in the secret places of our heart than He is in the length of our skirts.

Teenagers fear being "too different." Of course,

we must be careful and dress in good taste. We have to consider what is modest dress and what is not. A good general rule is, "If the Lord came, would I be ashamed of my dress?" or in regard to being somewhere, "If the Lord came, would I be ashamed of being here?"

God instructs us to be honest, that all liars shall have their part in the lake of fire, and here in my life, I realized I wasn't being honest. I wasn't doing what I felt the Lord really wanted me to do. I was listening to people instead of to God.

Young people must listen to God, too. They should be careful to follow the leading of the Holy Spirit, not striving to be different or do their own thing out of resentment or rebellion.

The Lord will direct any teenager who *earnestly* seeks Him. Then, as long as you're not doing something that you feel God is displeased with and is not contrary to the Word of God, step out and be yourself.

Chapter 4

MARRIAGE-AGE FEARS

I am a person who likes people and likes to be around them. But, you know, being around people creates problems. We sometimes feel like people are trying to force us into certain molds and roles that we don't like. Even our mates try to change us in ways that we do not want.

We Christians have a lot to learn about relationships. We have to start admitting the problems and facing the fears that we have with other people. If we can't be honest with other Christians, how can we be honest and upright in the world?

Jim and I recently had an honesty session with each other because we were beginning to have some problems in our marriage. We decided to take a week off, and we went to the hills of Arkansas just to be alone.

We hardly knew where to start because we really had not been communicating with each other in such a long time. We had to start somewhere, so we decided to make lists of what bothered us about each other and also lists of what we liked about each other. Then we prayed, discussed, blew up, laughed, cried, yelled, and prayed again—and *wow*! The results have been wonderful.

The Scripture tells us in James 5:16, **"Confess your faults one to another, and pray one for another, that ye may be healed."**

People, that is what Jim and I did. We got down to the bottom line. If the truth was to set us "free," we were going to put it to the test.

Satan tries constantly to keep us from being honest with our mates, and the end result is that we grow farther and farther apart.

We have also been taking some surveys of what really bothers other people and what their fears really are. We share four with you—two men and two women.

Male—married

"Who am I?" is a question that I had to face about six months ago when this image of myself that has been deeply steeped in the "born again" success philosophy and the success motivation of our society came crumbling down. Today I could not tell you that I am really completely in touch with the real me, but I can say that reality seems to be coming. All my life I have tried to live up to the standards that have been set before me and measure up to them, but I have not always been able to accomplish that. I believe that I've felt that if people saw what was really me that they would not like what they saw.

More than ever before I have a desire to be in touch with who I am and to be able to accept that person just as he is—to be able to be completely honest about myself and with other people. Many times I hurt inside and feel lonely as if no one really understands, not even my wife. I believe that this is intensified because I do not always understand myself. I do have a strong desire to be successful—but what is real success??

The church has one standard; the world, another. But how does this relate to me? In being very honest, I have been very disillusioned about the church and Christian organizations. Where is the reality? When are things going to begin to be "Christian"? So many people have been terribly hurt in these situations, including myself.

Personally, as a man I still battle with lust, and it is something I really wish wouldn't happen, but it does. I have had fear of failure, but recently had a real good failure and found that it wasn't the end of the world, so maybe next time won't be so bad. Sometimes I worry about losing my hair and getting older (men are vain too!). Sexually, I sometimes feel that I am not performing very well in my marriage. These are all things that I have begun to be honest with about myself. I have been beginning to feel a freedom—but does it ever all really come?

Male—single
1) I am afraid of not being loved.
2) I am always trying to make people like me.
3) I want to be able to love with Christ's love.
4) I am afraid of people really getting to know me.
5) I never feel I am good enough to work for the Lord.
6) I feel frustrated because of the things our Christian sisters and brothers do to each other in the name of God.
7) I get angry because some people get promotions and pay raises when others deserve them more.

8) I am afraid of being alone.
9) I am afraid that people will find out I can't do everything they ask.
10) I have a very strong will.
11) I feel as if I have very little to offer in the way of talent.
12) I love to sing, but I am scared to death when I do.
13) I am scared in front of a crowd.
14) I stretch the truth at times—I always ask forgiveness.
15) I love God, but I sure rebel sometimes.
16) I don't always understand why I have to go through so much.
17) I am stubborn.
18) I scream sometimes.
19) I am afraid my children won't love and respect me.
20) I cry easily.
21) I put on a front of hardness.
22) I cuss sometimes when I am angry.
23) I long for a closer walk with God.
24) I can't put my feelings into words when I am around "authority."
25) I carry resentment sometimes.
26) I am jealous at times.
27) I feel people don't like me.
28) Everyone is better than me.

Woman—married

I am very soft-hearted. So many things I see hit me hard, yet many others don't seem to mind them—even dumb things like a dead dog or people deformed. I even cry when I'm watching TV and a dog dies.

I have tried to keep the channels open with my husband. I realize that total marriage (oneness) comes when you feel all. We have a sex problem that probably is not uncommon—he can't stand my body because I'm fat. But I have been dieting, and he's starting to have sex with me again. It was hard to face that I kept myself a virgin all my unmarried life and suddenly I'm left without sex anyway. But he and I talked. It's not that he doesn't love me; he just has a problem to solve. I am trying to do my part, and now I don't care if he cannot change. I love him and must stick by him and show him I love him so he can change, too.

I have always wanted to be a writer. I enjoy sitting down and writing stories. But since I've been married, I haven't written anything. I do feel stifled anyway, not because of my husband, but because of his parents whom we live with. I can't write unless it's quiet. His dad plays the organ all the time, and his mother watches TV. So I hear noise all the time, and I even go to our room—but that crazy loud organ still goes on. Writing is one thing in my life I'm proud of—something I feel I can do well.

I'm not a jealous-type person. I'm proud of that, too. We hear so much about jealousy that I can't understand why people can't just be happy being with each other. To be honest with yourself is the most fulfilling thing in life. I have to get after me a lot. I usually do this in the car, and I cry, sob, worry, pray, and feel better about myself.

My mother taught me this. When I was younger and my parents divorced, I hated the world and was bitter about everything. But through her great love and understanding, I, too, found I was not the only person with a problem in this world. So, I have tried with, I think, much success to live my life in reality to myself. It works.

I can't stand hypocritical people who say they don't gossip, and they gossip talking about others that gossip. I try to look at the best in everyone. My mother taught me that, too. Once you love yourself, others can love you, too. I want to love people, but their "don't touch me" attitude gets me sometimes. But I try to help someone, and I pray that God will give me the ability to understand them.

Woman—single

First of all, I know I'm where I am in life because Jesus wants me here, but I don't know why. I'm scared of my future because I'm afraid I might do something wrong that isn't in God's will. I don't really feel like anyone really cares where I go or what I do—just so that it won't embarrass them. I'm trying to find my place in life, but I can't seem to find the right door. I'm scared of trying certain things because I'll probably fail.

I have a guy, back home where I'm from, that I think I really care for, but I'm not sure because I'm scared to show my real feelings towards him. He might just take it all for granted and not care at all. I know I've been putting him before what God's telling me to do, and I'm trying to fight it, but I can't seem to overcome it completely. When I think I have the victory, I fall right back to where I first began. I feel like I'm in a bondage to him.

I'm scared of marriage because I know it's so important to find the "right one." And I just don't know if I'll be going by my own feelings or what Jesus is telling me. How can I really know what Jesus wants me to do in all things? Will I ever know? Maybe, maybe not.

I have a fantastic (all Christian) family, and I love everyone of them deeply. But I find it hard to let them know how I really feel about certain things because they will probably preach at me and tell me what I "should" be doing instead of solving the immediate problem of why I do what I do.

I, a lot of times, feel like a real loser. Why would Jesus even want me? I never seem to obey Him. I always seem to put my desires before Him. If I really love Him like I say I do, would I treat Him like that?

I try fitting in with my friends by being a "happy, cheerful little Christian." But even that backfires on me because I'm accused of being a "flirt" with the guys. Can't I ever do anything right? There must be some medium between being a flirt or being stuck-up, so I could make everyone happy.

I guess to sum this thing up, I'd have to say I'm lonely down deep and searching for someone that will listen to me and understand me. Someone that would love me the way I am and not that I have to do certain things for them to love me. I know Jesus is there, but I need someone who I can physically see. I only want to be me and have people accept me that way.

Do some of these comments ring a bell? They certainly did with me, and, friends, we *must* face these problems in our lives and run to the roar. Jesus is truly the answer!

I think one of the hardest things to be as a Christian is a pastor's wife. I never wanted to be a pastor's wife because I'm the type of person who does not like to stay in one place and work in one place very long. I have always felt sorry for the pastors' wives. Most of the pastors' wives I knew had a houseful of little snotty-nosed kids and worked their fingers to the bone all the time. They had to make it to prayer meeting, Sunday morning service, Sunday night service, and every other meeting and usually had to drag all those little kids with them.

I never have wanted to settle down into a church. I guess I feared God would call me into that, but He never did. I have a great respect for pastors' wives. Pastors' wives live in fear a lot because of the fact they have to live, dress, talk, and walk for their husband's congregation. They're afraid that they're not going to raise their children just right, and if their children do something, the congregation isn't going to like it.

I would say probably fifty percent of the pastors' wives live in fear that they, or one of their children, are going to do something to disgrace the congregation, and they'll lose their church over it. And that's a terrible fear to have! We should not have to live up to what people think. I believe when we put fear aside and be what God created us to be, then we can really minister.

We must be what God has created us to be and not live in fear of not being what somebody else wants us to be all the time. That is true in our marriages. We must learn to accept each other as God made us or what He is changing us to be. When most of us are married, we have all sorts of hidden fears that as husbands and wives we need to discuss with each other.

I used to be terribly jealous of Jim because of the position that he had of interviewing so many women. He is handsome and has good manners, and I used to think that every talented young woman that walked through the door was making a pass at my husband,

and that was a very real fear to me. I knew that I was a very loyal person to Jim, and I prayed that he was to me.

"But, you know you're never sure," so says Satan. You hear so much about men, and everyone says that all men are sex maniacs. I had heard so much from so many people, and then I remembered how my dad left my mother. I think that is what made me not quite trust.

I finally had to come to the point where I made up my mind that I was going to trust Jim with those beautiful, young, talented women. That was something God and I just literally had to work out. I mean literally!! I had to pray and cry and scream it out. I screamed at Jim. I prayed. I cried, and I had to work it out through prayer and asking God to please, please, please take care of it and not let anything happen. God gave me a total victory over that, and I have not worried about it since.

Praise God, I don't feel that jealousy any more. Jealousy is a terrible thing, and it's brought on by fear. And jealousy is what destroys more people in our nation than anyone could imagine. It's pure somebody else succeeding—even your mates.

Another problem is that we want our mates to be what we want them to be and not what God wants them to be. We have a dream, and we want to fulfill that dream; and sometimes our dreams don't always coincide with what God has for us to do.

Jim and I were on the evangelistic field for over five years, and I was so afraid that we were never going to have a home. I kept thinking, "I will never have a home, and so I will never have children." I was afraid that I would never be able to have children because Jim did not want children while we were moving around on the evangelistic field. Then when we got into television, again, we were too busy to have children. I lived in a constant fear that we would never be able to have children.

Then when I finally did have children, I was afraid to totally give them to God.

When Tammy Sue came into our lives after we had been married for nine years, she was the most precious little bundle of joy. She looked like a Chinese doll, and she was absolutely beautiful and a perfect child. I did not get her dedicated for a long time, and I didn't really discuss it with Jim as to why; but in my heart I thought, "If I give her to the Lord, He'll take her away from me." I thought she would get sick and die. Yes, I thought she would die if I gave her to God. For the longest time, I couldn't settle that spirit in my mind.

As a result, Tammy Sue was dedicated at quite a late age because I really believe that you've got to be careful when you say something to God. I've always been very fearful of singing a song that tells the Lord to try me or to take me through trials. I never would sing a song like that because I knew I was talking to God, and I didn't want to have to go through those deep waters. I was frightened of those deep waters.

When I finally gave Tammy Sue to Jesus, I felt the greatest peace I've ever had come over me. Then I could trust Him to take care of her when I wasn't around. The fear turned around on me until it was a wonderously good thing instead of something that I'd worried about all the time.

Every now and then I would think of how God tried Abraham in the Scripture. Here was Abraham who had lived all these years loving the Lord. He was over a hundred years old and finally had the child of the promise. He has gone through so many trials and has proved to God over and over again that he loved Him. And even in his old age, in his old, old age, God says to him, "Abraham. . . ." God calls Abraham to prove again that he loves Him.

And I told Jim that Abraham has such a horrible trial, the horrible way he is going to have to prove to God that he loves Him—by taking his only son, the one that God had given him at an old age, and placing him on the altar to stick a knife in him.

I said, "Doesn't God ever trust us? Doesn't He ever know that we love Him enough? Won't we ever get rest from the trials of this world?"

And Jim said, "No. We aren't going to be able to rest until we get to heaven."

That really frustrated me to think that there is not a point in our lives that God trusts us enough that we won't ever have any more trials. As I thought about it more, though, I began to realize that God's trials were there to increase our faith. God wanted us to discover trust for ourselves. He wanted us to learn what really trusting Him means so that we could walk in a relationship built on trust.

I can just imagine Abraham walking up there and the little boy asking, "But Daddy, where is the sacrifice?"

I really feel Abraham knew God so well and served Him and had such great faith and lack of fear in what God might do that he could be obedient to God's directions even if it might mean his own son's death. Abraham knew and loved God. He knew God's patterns. He knew what God would do would be best! That's what we must do—really get to *know* God!

Abraham has Isaac on the altar and is just about to plunge that knife into him when the Lord tells him to lay the knife down and instead sacrifice a ram that's caught in the thicket. Isaac's mind must have been racing as fast as Abraham's about this time. Abraham was gambling his son's life that the Heavenly Father would do the right thing.

Both Abraham and Isaac had won the trust test. God must have been so pleased. Not only did Abraham prove his trust to God, but Isaac, the future father of Israel, showed that he knew what trust was, too. I bet they had a real victory celebration when they got home.

Satan had a double defeat! Both Abraham and Isaac trusted God despite all that Satan must have whispered in their ears. They ran to the roar and discovered that God really loved them.

Then there is the precious story of Moses that I would also like to share.

If a mother ever had something to fear, it must have been Moses' mother. This poor woman had to hide her baby because Pharoah had declared that all the male Israelite children were to be killed when they were born. So for three months Moses' mother hid the infant. But her faith in God was stronger than Pharoah's acts, according to Hebrews 11:23.

Imagine how hard it must have been to keep that suckling baby from being discovered. Every whimper and every cry could have brought panic to the household.

And her heart must have ached every time she thought of having to get rid of the baby. I can imagine her thoughts as she prepared a little boat to put the infant in to let it drift to God knows where. What if it drowns? What if an animal would get it? My little baby that I carried nine months, that I held to my breast and loved, now must be sent away. It's not fair, not right. Why, God? I've had him three months. Oh, please, let me keep him!

But she had to trust him into God's hands; she had no other choice. So she sent her daughter to the river with the baby and waited for her daughter's return. What would be the report? A crocodile got the baby, the Nile was full of them. A wave tipped over the tiny boat. An Egyptian found the babe and killed it.

But, no, the Lord had other plans for this baby and his trusting mother. God worked out one of His coincidences. Pharoah's daughter just happened to be passing by and heard the baby's cries. She picked up the infant and fell in love with it. Glory to God! Baby Moses was going to have a home and live like a king!!

If Moses' mother got that news, it would have been exciting enough, but there was even something better. Moses' sister approached the Pharoah's daughter and asked if she would need a nurse to take care of the baby for awhile. And sure enough, the Pharoah's daughter did. And do you know who became the baby's nurse? Why Moses' own mother. His own mother got to take Moses back home and care for her son and bring him to the royal palace and show him off once in awhile.

Wow, that's just like God. Out of our desperation He creates blessing. In our fear He provides a way of escape. Moses' mother had to run to the roar; she had to give her child up to God's care and trust Him for the answer. She faced her fears and the lion's roar and put Moses into God's hands. And the result was that she got to keep her child.

And one more thing. She got paid for her troubles. That's right, she got paid to take care of her own child. Talk about turning disaster into victory. This mother gave her child into the Lord's hands, and the Lord poured blessings down on her.

It truly is the step of absolute faith in a wonderful and loving God that overcomes our every fear.

It is so very important that we realize that we serve a loving and compassionate God who will never harm us but keep us always in His tender care.

One day God showed me, through Tammy Sue, how much He loved us. She had a little blanket that she sucked her thumb with. She had it ever since she was just a baby two days old. She'd take that little pink blanket with a narrow satin edge on it and hold it for security. Every time she sucked her thumb, she would turn the blanket all the way around until she found just the right edge.

One Sunday we all went to church, and I left Tammy Sue's blanket; and I think I cried harder than Tammy Sue after we realized the blanket was still at the church. She cried just for a few minutes about her blanket and then turned over and finally went to sleep without it. I, however, cried into the night, thinking, I have left that little baby's blanket. I was really more hurt by leaving her blanket at the church than she was. I took it harder than she did.

God spoke to me and said, "Tammy Sue loves that little blanket. You wanted her to have that little blanket so bad simply because she loves it so much. It hurt you even more than it hurt her for her not having that little blanket for one night. Tammy, now look at her. Would I take her away from you, knowing how much you love her and how much she means to you? I love you more than you love that little girl, and here you've cried half the night over her not having her little blanket." I really have not worried about my children since then.

One of my girlfriends and I were pregnant at the

same time. Our babies were to be born just about the same time. I gave birth to Jamie Charles about two weeks before Carolyn was to have her baby. We were away in Florida when we got the call from Carolyn's husband who through sobs said that she had had a baby boy but that he was dying.

All during her pregnancy we had talked about how wonderful it was going to be to have a little boy. We'd take them shopping together and all. But Carolyn's little boy died.

I could hardly handle this, and I said, "God, how could You do that to Carolyn?"

God spoke to me and said, "Because I knew you weren't strong enough to handle it. You couldn't have taken it, Tammy, but she could."

God knows what we can take, and I learned a lesson. He knows how much we can take and if we can bear the death of a child.

The Bible says God will not test us more than we can take. Look what he did to Job. He knew that Job would stand and could overcome his wife's comment, "Just curse God and die; you're so miserable."

Job looks up and he says, "Though God slay me, yet I'll trust Him."

God knew the heart of Job—just as He knows our heart.

I couldn't even look at Carolyn. I couldn't even talk to her, and she'd say, "Tammy, please, please don't be afraid to show me your baby. Please, don't be afraid to talk to me."

If I would have had two babies, I would have given her one. I hurt so bad for Carolyn. I hurt so desperately for her. I said, "You know, God, I couldn't have taken that."

God replied in my heart, "Tammy, I know you

couldn't have taken it, so I didn't put it on you."

Now Carolyn has had another baby, and God gave her a little boy that was just like the one that died. And he's perfectly healthy. And do they have a testimony! They are winning more souls to the Lord because that little baby died than they could have ever have won any other way.

Therefore, we don't need to fear what comes into our lives when we truly, truly believe that Scripture in Romans 8:28, **"And we know that all things work together for good to them that love God, to them who are the called according to his purpose."**

Fear is not of God. It's of Satan. The Bible says that fear and faith can't dwell in the same temple. I used to fear crib death. Doctors don't know what causes it. It even hit our PTL family. One of the engineers at PTL and his wife walked in their child's room and found their baby dead in its crib. No cause at all could they find. What a horrible fear. I used to live in fear that Tammy Sue would die with crib death. I'd walk to her room in the middle of the night listening to her breathing, checking on her. People, we must live the Word of God! We must say, "God, that child is yours; it belongs to you. Our lives are yours."

Friends sometimes can really unknowingly bring fear to us, too. A good example of that was when I was pregnant with Jamie Charles.

I had had such a wonderful pregnancy with Tammy Sue and thought this one also would be perfect. Anytime any girl would moan and groan and be sick through pregnancy, I didn't have any sympathy for her at all. I thought that was foolishness and all in her head.

A few weeks after I got pregnant, I began to go through the worst sickness I had ever experienced. I could not eat. I could not even take one bite of food. If I did, for two or three hours I'd be in bed doubled in a ball praying that God wouldn't let me die. My back felt like knives were stuck in it, and my chest felt like I was going to smother to death. I went to the doctor and said, "I don't know what's the matter with me. I'm just terribly, terribly sick." He couldn't do anything for me. All through my pregnancy I was sick.

On top of this, Jim was busy building Heritage Village and was gone all of the time and couldn't even be there to sympathize with me, or even help me. The house we lived in was fairly close to the PTL Club, but Heritage Village was thirty-three miles away. If Jim came home, it was a forty-five minute drive. He'd be gone until two or three o'clock in the morning sometimes. Here I would be at home sick and thinking he didn't care. I began to build up real resentment.

On top of all of that, one of the girlfriends had a dream. She dreamed that there was this funeral and Jim was standing up on a hillside holding a little baby boy. Tammy Sue was standing by his side, and there were lines and lines of people coming to see me at my funeral. She dreamed I would die in childbirth. I was about two months pregnant when she told me that dream.

I did not dare tell anyone this dream because I thought they'd think I was crazy to even think about it. It was on my mind all the time. Maybe I was going to die having this baby. Sick as I was, the Lord knows, I sure felt like dying. Almost every day was torture.

I felt Jim should care as much about me as he did about that building project. I just had to fight for any time I got with Jim. One night he didn't come home until about three o'clock in the morning; I had called and called PTL, but at that time there was seldom anyone there to answer the telephone. So, no matter how long I'd call, I'd not get an answer. All I could think of was that Jim's car had run off the road and he was somewhere hurt or dead.

Sometimes if someone would answer the telephone, they would say, "Jim left an hour ago." He left all right, but was standing in the parking lot for hours at a time talking and all excited about the building, like any man would be.

I thought Jim didn't care, that I was a second spot to him. I just could take no more. This was three or four weeks before Jamie was born.

When Jim came in that night at 3 A.M., I took one look at him, walked into the guest bedroom, and shut the door. I would not talk to him. He tried to tell me why he had been late, and I wasn't interested. I thought, "That doesn't make any difference to me. You don't care. That's it!"

I couldn't sleep, and the thought that he was upstairs sleeping made me madder than ever. At least he ought to be miserable, too. Come to find out, he was miserable, too. Terribly miserable.

The next morning I wouldn't speak to him. He went to work. That was something that had never happened in our marriage before, not ever. Just before the PTL Club was to come on, I got a telephone call from one of the men, "Tammy, Jim's here and he's crying. He's almost out of his mind worried about you. He loves you so much. He didn't realize what he was doing to you by not being with you when you needed him. Unless you two make things right, he's not going to be able to go on the air."

I felt so terrible and ashamed. Jim came to the phone, and I told him I was sorry. He said he was sorry and that he would pay more attention to me.

"Jim, I won't demand as much attention from now on, I promise you," I said. So we had a love affair over the telephone. I couldn't wait until he got home that night to hug and kiss him and say, "It's going to be all right."

The next day I went to sing on the PTL Club. I was so sick I could hardly stand up to sing, but I'd made up my mind that I was going to do it. Always in my heart my ministry comes before anything else. So, instead of standing, I sat down to sing, and still felt very sick. I finally said to the TV audience, "People, I'm sick and I can't get ahold of God for healing. I've got to have somebody help me. Will you please pray for me that the Lord will touch me and make these last couple of weeks of my pregnancy bearable? I don't know what to do or where to turn." Then I sang my song.

I was told prayer meetings rose up all over the United States. Praise the Lord, God touched me! I could now eat without getting terribly sick. I had only gained two pounds during the pregnancy up to that time, because I was so sick.

Jim began to pray that the baby would come before Christmas so I could be at home for Christmas Eve with Tammy Sue. I knew God was able to do that. It is so wonderful how God cares about the little things. It doesn't have to be a big thing with God. He's concerned about all the little tiny things in our life, and that's why I love Him so much. Our prayer was that God would bring the baby either before Christmas or wait until after.

Just a few days before Christmas I began getting little cramps at the bottom of my tummy, and I realized the time had come that I was going to have my baby. At 5 A.M. I awakened Jim. "Honey, I think we'd better go to the hospital." I had had bad high blood pressure for the last two weeks.

When we called the doctor, he said, "Due to your high blood pressure, you'd better come in right away."

We called Roger and Linda Wilson and they met us at the hospital. They took Tammy Sue. Tears came to my eyes as Tammy Sue left me, not knowing if I would ever see her again. Then the nurse wheeled me into the labor room.

Jim stayed with me until it was about time to do the program.

The doctor talked about a Caesarean section because I was in labor so long the previous time. He thought it might be another two-day ordeal for me if he waited. He talked to Jim about this, and Jim said, "Yes, I think we ought to go ahead with it."

Jim asked me, "Would you like me to stay here and have someone else do the PTL Club?"

I'd never had anything like this before, but the strength of God came into me and I said, "No, Jim, you go and do your work for Jesus, and Jesus and I will have this baby."

My blood pressure kept going up and up so they prepared me and took me into the operating room. I'd never been in an operating room in my life. Here I was, not a stitch of clothing on, stark naked, with my legs propped up in the air the way they do . . . the whole works . . . with all these people meeting me.

The doctor introduced me to the man who was putting the solution in my arm to put me to sleep. The doctor wanted me to meet him because he watched PTL. The room was also filled with nurses who watched PTL, waiting to see what we would have. In the midst of all this I had a peace and wasn't terrified like I was when I had Tammy Sue. I thought I would be terrified, and that maybe this was the last day I'd be on earth (because of that stupid dream), but I experienced what the Bible talks about when it says, "a peace that passeth all understanding."

"Tammy, are you ready?" the doctor asked.

When I woke up, I was on the table and the doctor was telling me, "Mrs. Bakker, you have a beautiful baby boy!"

I just started crying and saying, "Thank you, Jesus! Thank you, Jesus!"

The doctor called PTL. "Tammy's had her baby and it's a boy!" he told them. So the crew wrote on this big cue card: IT'S A BOY and flashed it in front of the camera, and the place went wild. People were cheering, jumping, and shouting: "They got their boy!" So everyone knew before Jim, who had left PTL and was on the way to the hospital after the show.

When Jim got to the hospital, the doctor told him he had a baby boy. The doctor said Jim laughed with a holy laughter. He laughed and laughed and laughed. The presence of the Lord just came over him.

Then Jim came to find out how I was doing. For a change, I was doing fine.

And what day did I come home? Christmas Eve! I spent Christmas Eve at home. In faith believing, I had bought a tiny red stocking and hung it on the fireplace next to Tammy Sue's.

Our whole little family celebrated with little Jamie Charles—Uncle Henry and Aunt Susan Harrison (how Jim and I love those two!) were with us also.

When we first got home, Tammy Sue walked up to Jamie Charles, looked at him, then to me and asked, "Mommy, is Jamie a Christian? Does he love Jesus?" And before I could answer her she put her little hand on Jamie and said, "Dear Jesus, come into Jamie's heart." She then looked at me and said, "It's all right now. We all love Jesus." What a precious Christmas!

Another fear many Christians have, besides losing their children, is losing their possessions. I never feared losing anything in television until the first time we lost it. I had never even thought about losing a television station. However, once we lost it, that seed of fear was again planted. If you plant corn, you're not going to get turnips, you know. If you plant corn, you're going to get corn, and that seed of fear was dropped in my heart by Satan. Until this day, I fear people coming into the television station and because of their jealousy, trying to take over PTL. I really have to cover that fear with the blood of Jesus.

Then there is always the side of television that it's such a horribly expensive vehicle, and you're always concerned and ask the question, "Is a million dollars going to come in this week?" I dare not think about or dwell on it. I just commit it to the Lord and say, "Well, Lord, You know our needs." Jim and I have both actually come to the place where we said, "If You want it Lord, take it."

And then the fear is not on us any more. It's passed off onto Jesus. We have to come to the place where we cast our cares on the Lord. The best way to get rid of fear is to go ahead and do what you're afraid of. Face it head on. Run to the roar.

Anything that you grab for, you're going to lose. It's like the little boy who puts his hand in the cookie jar and wants to take five cookies all at once. He can't get his hand out of the jar without opening his hand and dropping some of them. So he gets none. If he'd reach in and take out one cookie at a time, then he'd get every one he wanted. Praise God, "The battle is the Lord's."

Chapter 5

FAITH AND FEAR DON'T MIX

Something that I recently discovered that's been really eye-opening to me is Revelation 21:8. **"But the fearful, and unbelieving, and the abominable, and murderers, and whoremongers, and sorcerers, and idolaters, and all liars, shall have their part in the lake which burneth with fire and brimstone: which is the second death."** I have read that verse a number of times, and I've heard many sermons from that verse, but never once had I realized that *fear* was the first one on the list. The fearful are going to find their place in hell which is burning with fire and brimstone, which is the second death.

When I read that, it almost took my breath away. I had never read that before with the Holy Spirit's understanding. The fearful are listed with unbelieving, abominable, murderers, whoremongers, sorcerers, idolaters, and liars. So I began to ask myself why would God put the fearful in the very beginning of that verse.

Then I realized that just as hate is the opposite of love, fear is the opposite of faith. The Bible says in Hebrews 11:6, **"But without faith it is impossible to** please him...." If fear is the opposite of faith, with fear then it is impossible for us to see God. When we refuse to do something because of fear, we are in fact saying, "God, I do not trust You!" Now, God honors our trusting Him. He honors faith. Fear dishonors God; faith honors God.

Satan plans and plants fear. When we first hear the little ping of a fearful thought sound off in our brain, we've got to remember instantly that it's not from God. Fear never is from God.

The Holy Spirit gives us everything that is opposite to fear. The Word states in Galatians 5:22-23, **"But the fruit of the Spirit is love, joy, peace, long-suffering, gentleness, goodness, faith, meekness, temperance: against such there is no law."** God does not give us fear, according to 2 Timothy 1:7, **"For God hath not given us the spirit of fear; but of power, and of love, and of a sound mind."**

Fear is from the devil. There are fears of every description: fear of not being accepted; fear of not being a good wife, a good mother, a good husband; fear of not having the right kind of house. How many times were you going to ask somebody over to your house, and you decided not to because you were afraid they would not like it; or it was too messy, and they would talk about you. Or maybe you were afraid that your house wasn't right or your furniture wasn't new enough, or they might see a tear in the rug.

How many times we have let this fear grip us. Most of us will not even trust somebody as a friend because we are afraid that if they really knew us, they would not have anything to do with us. We have probably missed many very good friendships with a lot of people because of this fear.

Many people are afraid to leave the house because

they won't know what is going to happen. They are afraid to fly or afraid to drive.

I got a letter from a lady the other day, and she was frantic because she was going to have to fly for the first time. Her husband wanted to take her to Hawaii for their twenty-fifth wedding anniversary. She called the PTL prayer line, and crying, asked for prayer. Then she sat down and wrote me a letter, and she stated she was going to fake a sickness so she didn't have to go. She also didn't want her husband to realize how deathly afraid she was of flying.

I decided the Lord would have me call her, and I did the day before she was to leave. I told her the lion story and how that she should run to the roar and just get on the airplane, giving praise to Jesus. I said to her, "Isn't it wonderful that God grounded all the DC-10's so He could have them fixed just for us?" She took her trip and later wrote me and sent us twenty dollars so we could make a phone call to someone else who was afraid of flying because she enjoyed her trip so much to Hawaii. She had a story of real victory.

Some people are afraid to go to sleep at night or even get out of bed in the morning. There is an unbelievable amount of fears. 1 John 4:18 says that **"perfect love casteth out fear."** Fear is also the opposite of love. There is something wrong in our lives if we are filled with fear. It is obvious that there is also something wrong in our love life with Jesus. If we are fearful all the time and do not know what to do because of fear, we had better look into our relationship with God, because there's something wrong! You don't fear someone that you trust so totally.

When I was a little girl and I would walk somewhere in the dark with my daddy, I had no fear because I loved him and knew that he was going to take care of me. When I'm walking down the street with Jim, I have no fear. However, if I'm walking by myself, I might be a little bit worried that someone is going to come and snatch my purse, or someone is going to come up behind me and grab me or something like that. But when I'm walking with Jim, I have no fear because I love him, and I trust him, and I know that he is going to take care of me.

The same should be true when we're walking with God. If we are in the right relationship with Him, we ought to have no fear. If we really know Him, we also know that He has never failed us yet and that He's going to take care of us and watch over us and protect us just like He said He would do in His Word. The verse says, "Perfect love casteth out fear!" **"Fear hath torment. He that feareth is not made perfect in love"** (1 John 4:18). The Bible says if we are made perfect in love, we will not be fearful. Isn't that exciting? Praise the Lord!

Jesus said in Mark 4:40, **"Why are ye so fearful? How is it that ye have no faith?"** Here we have it again. If you're fearful, you have no faith. Faith and fear do not mix. There is no possible way that you can mix faith and fear. If you have fear, then you don't have faith. Revelation 21:8 says, "But the fearful, and unbelieving . . . shall have their part in the lake which burneth with fire."

What happens to your faith when you get fearful? Faith leaves, and you tense up; you can't seem to reach out for God! You can see the lines in the faces of people who live in constant fear. Yes, you can see the fear lines etched in their faces. However, people who go around in faith with the peace of God on their face look entirely different. People of faith age differently than fearful people do. Their lines are gentler and softer. Cheer lines are different lines than the ordinary lines you get from aging.

Today when I look at my grandmother, she has aged so beautifully. She is eighty-four years old and hardly has any lines in her face because she has had the peace of God. She served Jesus and has loved Him and served Him! Then I look at people who have not known Jesus Christ as their personal Saviour. The lines in their faces look hard and bitter. It really makes a difference.

Fear comes daily to visit the lives of God's children. It comes to me in many forms—fear that our children are going to get sick, and if they do get sick, fear that it's going to get worse. Jim and I have various fears that hit us constantly because we're in a position where we're known nationwide. However, when all those fears well up to destroy our faith, I begin repeating Scriptures again and again, Scriptures on fear. Then that fear goes away and faith takes its place.

It's not sin to be tempted with fear just as long as you don't dwell on it and let it destroy you. It's like the old saying, "A bird can fly over your head, but you don't need to let it nest in your hair." So it's not wrong for a fearful thought to come over your mind, but you don't need to let it make a nest in your mind and ruin your faith.

Lord, deliver us from our little fears. We have so many little fears that stop us from being all that Jesus wants us to be. I say they're little, but, boy, when we're in that fearful situation, they're real. The fear is real. People say it's all in your mind.

I don't care if it is all in your mind; it's still real, and it's still a tormenting thing. I think fear is one of the biggest reasons that people have nervous breakdowns and one of the biggest reasons for heart attacks. I believe fear is a basic problem in America and the world today.

Fear of starvation, fear of losing your job, fear of not keeping up with the Joneses. Fear that you won't get the promotion or fear that your car is going to be wrecked.

There are a million little fears that can confront us. Satan loves to attack in the small areas of our lives. He can't take our salvation, so he tries to take our joy. He's no dummy; he's a bully who's trying to ruin our victory in Jesus.

Satan loves to take those little fears, those little things that we haven't trusted to Christ, and build them up. They build to the point of becoming phobias. There are all kinds of phobias from acrophobia (fear of height) and ailarophobia (fear of open spaces) to zoophobia (fear of animals). There's aquaphobia (water) and astraphobia (lightning); there's claustrophobia (closed spaces) and cynophobia (dogs); there's mysophobia (fear of dirt, germs, or contamination) and even numerophobia (fear of numbers).

God never promised us that we wouldn't have fear, but He did say that "perfect love casts out fear: because fear has torment." Boy, I know what torment is. We get so many calls at PTL from people who are living in fear. I remember this one lady who called for prayer for her son who was afraid of people. Her son was twenty-three years old, and he wouldn't even go out of the house.

Many things in our past contribute to our present fears, just like when I saw the plane accident and became afraid of flying. We hide our fear or ignore it when we're first afraid, but it gets bigger and bigger if we don't deal with it, and it finally comes out. It jumps out in a way we don't expect. The rest of our life can be as normal as good apple pie, but when that one fear situation comes up that we are afraid of, the fear takes over our life. It makes us obey it.

It's like the tail wagging the dog. The tail makes us walk down ten flights of stairs instead of taking the elevator. Or it makes us tell a little lie over the phone so that we don't have to meet new people at that party. It makes us pretend we're sick so that we don't have to complete the school work that we're afraid won't be good enough. It makes us turn on the TV to avoid thinking about a family problem.

The tail wags enough to make us go out of town on Sunday instead of seeing that person in church that we're afraid to talk to. It makes us avoid writing letters to someone who needs to hear from us because we're afraid they'll judge us for our bad spelling. That wagging tail of fear even makes us avoid being with other people because they might see the bumps on our face or the fat around our middle or the dandruff in our hair.

Satan keeps throwing fear at us. He is always testing our armor, and we have to battle those fears and run to the roar. When we win, Satan will attack with something else. Every time we win, though, we have gained some more ground! With Jesus as our commander we conquer those areas of our lives that Satan once held. The Bible says in Romans 8:37 that we're more than conquerors through Jesus. Jesus will help us win our fear battles.

I would like to say just turn your fear over to Jesus, and it will go away, but it doesn't work that way. Satan doesn't just go away and leave us alone. We have to win the battle daily. When Satan comes at me with fear that Tammy Sue will have trouble in school or something, I have to meet that fear head-on right away. I mean right away. If I don't, that fear will grow, and pretty soon, you know, I'll be walking in that fear.

I have to conquer that fear. And it feels good to be a conqueror, too. Maybe Satan doesn't leave us alone, but he sure does provide us with the chance to be conquerors through Jesus.

I think one reason Satan brings fear upon us in the first place is to make us so worried about ourselves that we can't even think of carrying out God's will in our lives. We say Jesus is the Victor, but then we look at our fears and don't believe it. We hear sermons on how Jesus is everything we need, but we look at our fears and feel like we haven't had a victory in years. Satan loves to get us distracted from God's will by making us look at our failures, and one way he does it is by making us see fearful areas in our lives instead of the victorious areas.

Something we have to remember is that with God we will continue to have victory. As we overcome fear, we can carry out God's will. Part of God's plan for us is to take fearful, resentful losers and transform them into worshipping, Word-confessing winners. God doesn't start with super-star Christians to accomplish spiritual exploits. He begins with simple people and does super things through them.

But first He must deal with the fear-producing issues in our lives. Look at Gideon in the book of Judges. This Israelite was like the rest of the nation and cowered before the oppressing Midianites. Yet he developed into the man who led one of the most stunning, dramatic victories in Israel's history.

Here Gideon was threshing wheat in secret behind

a winepress to hide it from the Midianites. The Israelites lived in constant fear at what the Midianites would do to them next. Gideon's enemy appeared too strong for him to do anything.

And while he worked in secret for fear of the Midianites, an angel of the Lord came to him according to Judges 6:12, and said, "The LORD is with thee, thou mighty man of valour." Imagine that, the angel called Gideon a man of valour while he was hiding for fear of the enemy. God saw Gideon's potential just like He sees our potential. Even though we may be afraid, God sees the victory we can have.

Gideon didn't realize what it meant to have God on his side, and he blamed God for his fears. Gideon said to the angel, "Oh, my Lord, if the LORD be with us, why then is all this befallen us? and where be all his miracles which our fathers told us of, saying, Did not the LORD bring us up from Egypt? but now the LORD hath forsaken us, and delivered us into the hands of the Midianites."

Gideon is so much like the rest of us. Here God comes to deliver him from the thing he fears most, and Gideon tells God off. Gideon's fears were bigger to Gideon than God's promises were! And if that wasn't enough, Gideon was a real self-confessed loser, too. He says to the angel, "Oh, my Lord, wherewith shall I save Israel? behold, my family is poor in Manasseh, and I am the least in my father's house."

Gideon sounds just like me speaking. "Why, God, I come from a little town in northern Minnesota. How can I have victory over my fear? My family is poor; I don't have great abilities. I'll never win. Oh, God, help me; I can't win the victory." But all the time God is there and says to me (if I would just listen) the same thing he said to Gideon. "Surely I will be with thee, and thou shalt smite the Midianites (my fears) as one man."

Gideon started to catch on. He started to see that God might have the answer after all. Gideon still had doubts and fears, but our patient Lord kept showing him that he could trust what God had said. God helped Gideon get 300 other men to come against an enemy that held the entire nation of Israel in bondage.

And what were the results? God gave Gideon an overwhelming victory. Judges 8:10 says that 120,000 Midianites died in the battle. Wow! 120,000 to nothing. That's some score. According to Judges 7:2, God intentionally made Gideon have only 300 men, so that Israel would glorify God, and not think that they had done it on their own. The same mighty God wants us to trust Him for victory over our fears today. We are weak, but He is strong. We don't see how we can conquer the fear, but Jesus sees that we have victory when we allow Him to be our commander. He sees our potential and says to us like he said to Gideon, "The LORD is with thee, thou mighty man of valour."

I think the apostle Peter was a little like Gideon, too. Christ saw Peter's potential in the same way that He had seen Gideon's. When Peter's brother introduced him to Jesus, Christ greeted him in John 1:42 with the declaration that Peter would one day be called a rock.

That's just like Jesus to look beyond our little lives and see who we can be when we walk with Him. I mean, here's Peter, a little fisherman, a man who was impulsive and who made all kinds of mistakes. But Jesus saw him through spiritual eyes. He saw this little nobody and knew what he would be.

Peter had lessons to learn, too. He was a fisherman. He had braced many a storm at sea, and his trust was in the sturdy fishing vessel he possessed.

In that boat Peter felt security. He knew how to steer into the teeth of the storm, confident that his vessel could mount each high wave and rise out of each deep trough. What did Peter have to fear in that boat—almost nothing!!

On one occasion, as the disciples were ferrying Jesus across the Sea of Galilee, a fierce storm arose. The great waves swept over the side of the ship until it seemed it must sink. Even Peter lost his trust in the boat. They called on Jesus to awaken from His sleep, and the Master calmed the storm. Peter must have learned a good lesson then about where his trust must be.

He's just like so many of us. We feel secure in our homes or our cars or our jobs and think that nothing can harm us. What do we have to fear? But then the storm comes, and we have to cry out to Jesus to save us. We see that the things we feel so secure in are not really going to save us at all, and that Jesus is the only One who can calm the storm of fear in our lives.

On a later occasion Christ sent His disciples to cross over the sea, promising them that He himself would follow later. Again a sudden storm arose, and the wind was so contrary that they could make no headway although they strained at the oars. The disciples were worried and afraid; after all, they didn't have the Master along to calm the sea this time.

But then an odd thing happened as recorded in Matthew 14. The disciples saw what they thought was a spirit, and according to Matthew 14:27, they actually "cried out for fear."

These men were so scared that they screamed. They didn't recognize the answer to their problems when He was actually coming to them. They had double fear—the storm and the "spirit."

Jesus knew their fear, though, and dealt with it.

"Straightway Jesus spake unto them, saying, Be of good cheer; it is I; be not afraid." Isn't that just like Jesus to speak to us and calm our hearts when we fear most. These men were even afraid of Jesus because they didn't recognize Him, but He spoke and calmed their hearts.

I think Peter must have learned a lesson from his other storm experience. He was willing to give up the security of his boat because he was going to go to the calmer of life's storms. Peter shouted out, "Lord, if it be thou, bid me come unto thee on the water."

And Jesus said, "Come."

So often it's hard for us to leave the security of things we know. We're afraid of the unknown. We might sink, we might fail, we might drown. But Christ tells us to come out of our earthly security and walk to Him. Peter had to face all these fears. He had heard Christ's voice, and now he just had to go to Him.

If I had written the Bible, I would have had Peter walk safely over the waves to Jesus and have them live happily ever after.

Christ had a greater purpose in mind. This Peter who would be a rock later now had to learn a little more about a spiritual walk. Peter stepped out of the boat with nothing but the word of Christ to sustain him. He was to attempt the impossible. The lake wasn't frozen three feet thick like northern Minnesota. It was a shaky, white-foamed menace stirred by a boisterous wind.

Then Peter goofed. Just like Tammy and other Christians so many times, Peter looked at the obstacles instead of at Christ. Down he went. He reminds me of myself. Jesus tells me to do something and I step out, but then I start looking around and start saying, "Hey, that's humanly impossible. I can't do that." I let Satan come in and huff and puff and stir up the waves, and I take my eyes off Christ. Down I go, and like Peter I have to cry out, "Lord, save me."

I start trying to do things in the flesh instead of in the Spirit and the waves swallow me up. Jesus is always there waiting for me to catch on. When Peter cried out, the Bible says that *immediately* Jesus stretched forth His hand and caught him." Hand in hand Jesus and Peter stepped to the boat.

"Why did you doubt?" Jesus asked.

Peter had learned a lesson in faith. His faith was not to be in his ship but in Jesus.

Later in life Peter would face a great multitude of people and again step out, trusting Jesus to give him words of life to speak to the very ones who had put Jesus to death. This time (on the day of Pentecost) there was no longer fear, no sinking beneath the waves. In Christ, Peter was a rock, a conqueror, a preacher who could bring such conviction to the multitude that they would cry out, "What must we do to be saved?"

Christ had given Peter a bath in the Sea of Galilee to teach Peter to trust Him. Christ wants us to trust Him, too. We can't listen to Satan when he blows contrary winds of fear our way. Satan tries to take all our little fears and make a big storm out of them. He tries to make us fear our fears instead of walking over the foamy water and through the whistling winds to Jesus.

Chapter 6

THE UNPARDONABLE SIN

I had a fear one time that I'd committed the unpardonable sin. I thought for sure I had, and for one entire year the devil tore me to pieces with fear that God would not forgive me. I would sob and cry, and I would say, "I don't even want to live if I've committed the unpardonable sin. I want to see Jesus. I want to see Jesus because I love Him so much."

Jim would come up to me and say, "Honey, the very fact that you love Jesus so much proves you haven't committed the unpardonable sin."

Yet, for one year, every single day, I pleaded the blood of Jesus over my mind. I'd say, "Jesus, I plead your blood. Cover me with your blood today."

I kept repeating Philippians 4:8, *"Finally, brethren, whatsoever things are true, whatsoever things are honest, whatsoever things are just, whatsoever things are pure, whatsoever things are lovely, whatsoever things are of good report; if there be any virtue, and if there be any praise, think on these things."* That verse saved me. I had to flood my mind with Jesus' thoughts so I wouldn't keep listening to what Satan told me.

There are many, many, many other people who think they've committed the unpardonable sin. They're sobbing, and they're crying out, "I love Jesus so much." They usually haven't committed the unpardonable sin; it's a trick of the devil. It's a seed that was planted that the devil made grow. We've got to be careful of the seeds of fear and doubt that are planted in our lives by Satan. It's not by God. Anything bad is from the devil. Good comes from the Lord. Encouragement comes from God—not fear and doubt and hurtful things.

Another thing, the more we dwell on the fear, the greater it grows. We are sure it is going to come to pass although it never does. For example, I had this crazy dream once, and when I woke up, fear gripped my heart. I dreamed that a man and his whole family were massacred in their home. That fear began to gnaw at me because I loved that man and his family so much. It was one of our people at PTL.

God spoke to my heart and said, "You resist that fear, and it will never happen." I did, and it never happened. I refused to dwell on that fear and to let it grow, and it died away.

Satan would just love for us to dwell on fear so that it occupies our whole lives. If we live in fear, we can't be living in God's freedom. Satan will do anything to keep us separated from God. He tries to diminish the victory that Christ won on the cross by making us fear that we haven't been forgiven of all our sins—just like when I was so worried I had committed the unpardonable sin.

I was afraid I was eternally separated from God. I didn't fully understand how forgiving God is. Many people in the Bible had to discover in personal ways that God still loved sinners; they didn't understand

God's ways, either.

Adam was the first one to experience God's love. Who in all creation was more blessed than he was? Created in God's own image, given a perfect body, he had a mind capable of receiving all truth and knowledge because his spirit was in unbroken fellowship with his Creator. He dwelt in a luxurious garden with plants and trees bearing fruit for food (what fruit that must have been!), pure crystal waters, birds, fish, animals to enjoy, and he even had a glorious woman to love and to be his ideal helper.

Adam also had limits set by God and the right to choose obedience or disobedience. When Eve was deceived and ate and offered the forbidden fruit to her husband, his disobedience was deliberate. Why did he partake? Was it to please his wife—or curiosity? Was it pride of self—premeditated rebellion—wanting to be like God?

Whatever the real motive, the fear that Adam felt as the full realization of his act came upon him must have been sickening. The realization of his nakedness—the entering in of self-conciousness, knowing his accountability to God and frantically trying to cover himself with fig leaves and then he and Eve hiding behind trees in the garden—what a sinking, sickening black void of fear he and Eve must have experienced! His fear was irrational—as if anyone could hide from God behind a tree; his fear was cowardly—when asked by God what he had done, he blamed his wife. How typical of all of us!

As he began to realize the extent of the consequences of his act—the broken fellowship with God, the disruption of harmony, the pain, toil, death—he must have been in total despair. Adam had to suffer the consequences of his act, but God put into motion the great solution to Adam's sin, fear, and despair. God planned the Perfect Sacrifice to cover all of men's sins. This was symbolized for Adam in the shedding of the blood of the animals that he must have loved, so that a loving God could provide Adam with a covering. Just think of that: not only did God plan a way out of the first sinner's problems, but He loved Adam and Eve enough to clothe them.

I would imagine that Satan hadn't bargained on God's great love. He probably hoped that Adam and Eve would have to join his ranks. But God loved man, even when he sinned, far more than Satan dreamed.

Satan tries to get us to the point where we don't think God will forgive us. When he gets us that far, we give up hope in life. I think many Christians today are on the verge of suicide because Satan has hoodwinked them into believing that God can't forgive their sin. We judge ourselves much harder than God judges us because we don't understand how much God always works in love.

Satan makes us think of only one side of God's character. Satan is so sly that he makes us forget we're alive today because of God's mercy and love. He makes us think that God's verdict will mean death. If we listen to Satan long enough, he is a good enough accusing attorney that we will become afraid of God. We end up punishing ourselves instead of throwing ourselves upon the mercy of God.

Just because we've not been faithful to God does not mean that God will not be faithful to us. All we have to do is call on Him. 1 John 1:9 says, **"If we confess our sins, he is faithful and just to forgive us our sins, and to cleanse us from all unrighteousness."**

King David knew what God's mercy was. In one of his psalms to the Lord in 1 Chronicles 16:34, he sings out, "O give thanks unto the Lord; for he is good; for his mercy endureth forever." That *forever* includes right now. Jim and I are walking in God's mercy right now, and so is everyone else. That old lion, Satan, tries to roar out something else at us so that we don't slow down enough to see God's love.

If we had to be perfect before God would love us, we'd all be doomed. I know many people who are saved but have "blown it" in some area of their lives. They commit some sin and walk around in guilt and fear. They forget that they are being perfected; they're not perfect yet. We can't fix ourselves up anyway; it's Jesus who has to do the fixing.

King David is a good example of someone who really messed up, but God still chose him to be the one Christ himself decended from. Here David is, the king of Israel, the one God raised up to have favor with the people. He is at the height of his popularity, and then he sees Bathsheba.

I can just see him sitting on his couch, not being able to go to sleep, fear gripping his heart. The shepherd boy who had written, "He giveth his beloved sleep," now could not sleep. I bet he thought that it would have been better if he would have been leading his men in battle away from the palace than to have seen Bathsheba bathing on her rooftop that day several months ago. He probably consoled himself with the thought that kings have rights, yes, even certain privileges that the common man doesn't. After all, he thought, he needed some relaxation; the pressures of his office were heavy.

Besides, what was Bathsheba doing bathing in open view if she did not want to be noticed and possibly even seduced? Oh, yes, he knew women could be very cunning. So, rationalizing away the blame and quieting his conscience, he tried again to fall back to sleep.

He knew that he had to see Joab, his faithful captain, in the morning. Something had to be done about Uriah, Bathsheba's husband. He had been away in battle and didn't know his wife was pregnant. All of David's plotting to conceal the pregnancy and his own part in it had failed. Now there was no choice but to get rid of Uriah by having Joab put him at the front of the battlefield.

Sin was leading to more sin, and David's fear of getting caught was leading him into more trouble. He was guilty before God, and rather than admitting his mistake and asking God's forgiveness, he was now adding murder to his sin list.

Satan must have been roaring in David's ear and prancing around in glee. He had David right where he wanted him—afraid of God and afraid of man. David would have to keep covering, keep going into more sin, keep running from God and himself.

God loved David too much to let him continue on his downward path. He sent the prophet Nathan to stop his sinning and face the consequences. David acknowledged his guilt and confessed that he had sinned against God.

David's plight is so much like ours. We sin against God and rather than running to God and confessing our sin and making things right, we listen to Satan as he leads us further and further away from God.

I get so mad at myself sometimes. I let these little things build up in my heart and don't take them to Jesus right away. Instead, I hide or ignore them. Satan then comes in and works me over and tries to make my failure seem so large. I should know I've got to cry out to God right away and get forgiveness so that Satan can't hold anything over on me.

It feels so good when I take it to the Lord. He replaces my fear with peace and my guilt with love. We're just like David. Despite our failures God loves us. In one of the Apostle Paul's sermons in Acts 13:22, he repeats what God had said about David. "I have found David the son of Jesse, a man after mine own heart, which shall fulfill all my will."

I see so many Christians at PTL and all over whose hearts are "after" God's own heart. All these precious people fulfill God's will as they ignore old Satan's roars about their sins and shortcomings and simply look to Jesus daily for His forgiveness and love.

There's another fear that can keep us from walking in God's will, too. That's our own ego problem of what others will think when we do what God tells us to do. Boy, has Satan attacked me with this fear. Being the co-host of PTL Club, I felt forced to act a certain way and play a certain role to be accepted by other Christians in my ministry.

It was hard to overcome trying to be accepted by others instead of seeing that God wants me to minister just as I am. God called me, Tammy Bakker, to serve Him. He didn't call me to conform to other people's opinions of how I should minister.

I don't mean that I should stay way out in left field and not listen to others. God works through others, especially Jim, to help guide and convict me, but I have stopped trying to please others simply to win their acceptance.

After all, the ministry is the Lord's, not mine. I often see people who come to PTL and act like all of God's work depends on them. Underneath, they're so unhappy. They end up trying to do God's work in the flesh instead of in the Spirit.

It reminds me of the story of Jonah. Jonah didn't really care for all those people in that great city of Nineveh. Jonah cared for Jonah. He was afraid of being made to seem the fool or the bad guy. Jonah wanted to be liked; he was afraid of being unpopular and not accepted.

Jonah didn't want to be rejected, so Jonah rejected God. Boy, does that hit home. He ran away, tried to escape, left town rather than doing God's work and facing the possible consequences.

I can hear him now say, "Oh, God, I don't want to go to Nineveh! You can save those people some other way. Why me, Lord? Please! You're a God of love; we don't have to bring this unpopular stuff up, do we? I mean, who would come to my church or home. I would never be invited out to dinner." But the consequences outside of God's will were even worse—that big old whale swallowed him. Talk about fear!! Going in that big fish's mouth must have been worse than any fear he had ever had before. Jonah cried out of his distress to the Lord, and He heard him.

Well, Jonah ended up in Nineveh after overcoming his fear of doing God's will. But Jonah had another lesson to learn. He still had to overcome his ego problem while doing God's will. He was still afraid of what others would think of him.

Jonah preached hard at Nineveh. He told the people that God's wrath was about to fall on their evil city. Jonah must have been some preacher, because the whole town responded. He must have had an altar call that some preachers would give their right arm for. They fasted and repented and God heard their cry. He forgave them and spared their city.

Poor Jonah—his ego really took a licking. He

forgot that God was sovereign and that he was just the messenger. He wanted to play God himself. He was afraid he would lose everyone's respect because judgment hadn't come the way he had preached. He was so afraid that he had lost *his* ministry that he actually asked God to take his life from him.

So often Satan works on us the same way he must have worked on Jonah. He places fear in us that we will lose our ministry or that we won't be accepted. All the time, I bet Jonah would have been the most loved man in Nineveh after the people repented because he was the messenger that saved their city.

Instead, he went outside the city and pouted because God had not worked the way Jonah wanted Him to. Jonah lost a great blessing because of his fears.

Satan must really laugh sometimes at how we act. I bet he really licks his chops when he sees we don't understand God's great love. He will try to put us in fear any time and any place he can. He will even bring us fear when we listen to sermons if he can. If he can keep our teaching unbalanced, we will act unbalanced and start to fear.

Then, even what we hear in church brings us fear. We hear all the time that we should fear the Lord, and we end up being afraid of Him. Imagine that, afraid of the Heavenly Father who loves us. I heard a lot of sermons about the fear of the Lord when I was a child, and I think that's why I sometimes can't understand His love now.

You just don't know the impression some of these sermons and teachings have on kids' lives. We can warp their whole future, even their love for God, if we do not give them a balance about who God is.

We end up fearing God just like we would fear a boogie man or a stranger. We're afraid He'll pounce on us if we sin, and we get scared of Him so much we can't love Him.

I've seen children, too, who think God is like their own father. Because He's called a father, they picture Him like they see their daddy. If their daddy is mean and unfair, kids think a little that that's how God is. I know of many Christians who can't understand God the Father because their own experience with a father was so bad. God isn't like some earthly father who comes home and picks on the wife and slaps the kids just because he has had a bad day.

That's really a warning to us parents to teach love and "walk in love," as Ephesians 5:2 says. You know, we're the Jesus our children see.

When the Bible tells us to fear God, it doesn't mean be afraid of God. If that was the case, David would never have written Psalm 34:4, **"I sought the Lord, and he heard me, and delivered me from all my fears."** David would be contradicting the rest of the Bible.

A person who has accepted Jesus into his life has nothing to fear from God. Punishment is reserved for the sinner, not for the saved. God corrects the saint but punishes the sinner. Hebrews 12:6 says, **"For whom the Lord loveth he chasteneth."** And it goes on to say that He does it "for our profit" and that the end result will be that it yields the "peaceable fruit of righteousness."

Isn't that just like our Heavenly Father to correct us and help us have righteousness in our lives as peaceable fruit coming forth. That's a far cry from what many of us were told about God when we were young in church. When the Bible tells us who are saved to fear God, it means that we should give the highest respect and reverence to Him because He has all power and all authority. We Christians really need a balance in our picture of our loving God.

Our loving Father doesn't withdraw Himself from us, either. If there's any separation, it's because we do it. When we "do our own thing," that's when we start becoming afraid of God. We reject what we know is right and become afraid of God ever finding out.

King Saul was a good example of this in the Old Testament. Saul was of the tribe of Benjamin and was a tall, handsome, and very humble man. God sent the prophet Samuel to anoint him king, and he warned Saul to never forget God.

But power, wealth, and success became Saul's gods, and his power went to his head. Humility gave place to pride. He willingly got away from God. Then he disobeyed God's specific command that he should destroy everything the Amalekites had. When Saul went to battle and defeated the Amalekites, he kept some of the valuables for himself.

Saul continued his downward spiral, and he lost God's favor. He must have known what fear is! Imagine realizing that God's favor was no longer on him—the God who had raised him up and given him power and blessings and honor was no longer close to him.

When we deliberately disobey God, a lot of fear will pour in where the love should have been. When we *deliberately* reject God, all we have left is "a certain fearful looking for of judgment and fiery indignation," as Hebrews 10:27 says.

I realize now that I wasn't deliberately rejecting God when Satan tried to tell me I was committing the unpardonable sin. That was Satan's trick. I knew of the judgment of God, but I hadn't balanced it with His tender mercies. Besides, God has promised us in Hebrews 13:5 that He will never leave nor forsake us. Satan always tries to put a wedge between us and God.

There aren't any Christian Sauls because Jesus is now the King of kings. Jesus forgives us because of His great love for us. I had to battle off Satan's lies and look to Jesus who took *all* of our sins (past, present, and future) to the cross. Jesus loves and forgives. We can't listen to Satan when he tells us something else.

Chapter 7

FEAR OF REJECTION

Psychologists call man a social animal. I don't know about the animal, but I sure agree with the social. I love to get out and be with people. I love busy stores and good times with people. It's just not much fun all by yourself. In order to have a party, you have to have guests.

Christ Himself was constantly surrounded by people. He must have had such a wonderful personality and love. People flocked to Him just to be in His presence. I would love to have sat on the mountain side to listen to Him as He spoke and then fed the five thousand. That must have been some church picnic!

Christ was social. He attended weddings, went to a tax collector's house for lunch, visited the sick, and had intimate communion with close friends. He was really involved in life. But that's why He came to earth in the first place.

God wanted a love relationship. You can't have love all by yourself. It takes two to have love. Otherwise, all you have is frustration.

To have love means you have to take a chance.

You have to risk something. God risked His only begotten Son so that He might have a love relationship with man and that His Son might have a bride. Jesus knew the price for love would be high. It would cost Him His life! But it was worth it to Christ. He knew the reward of love would be greater than anything else. Christ had a set goal; He would love at all costs. Nothing could stop or sidetrack Him as He set about to restore mankind to a love relationship with God.

Christ had many obstacles to overcome on the way to His goal, too. And wouldn't you know it, the devil was one of those big obstacles. Satan hates love. He will do anything in his power to pervert or destroy it.

As Jesus was about to start His ministry, that old lion, Satan, came by to change Christ's course. He tempted Christ in the wilderness to try to change God's plan. That's just like Satan to attack when a person's all alone. Christ was alone in the wilderness for forty days and then Satan comes to Him to tempt Him.

Satan offered Christ everything. In Matthew 4:8-9 the Bible records that Satan took Christ to a high mountain "and sheweth him all the kingdoms of the world, and the glory of them; and saith unto him, All these things will I give thee, if thou wilt fall down and worship me."

A lesser man than Christ might have jumped at the chance. I've seen many people give up a love relation with God for the chance to have wealth and glory. But Christ was different! He knew the consequences of following Satan. Even in His weakened condition from fasting forty days, Christ loved the Church so much that He commanded, "Get thee hence, Satan: for it is written, Thou shalt worship the Lord thy God, and him only shalt thou serve.''

I think most of us lose sight of our goal at times and listen to Satan and his temptations. We get in a church and want to love but lose sight of the goal. I have seen ministers and churches who start building bigger and better buildings and seem to get glory from man for awhile. But the end is that some of those big churches go broke or have a church split or something.

We in the ministry have to be so careful to keep the proper goal in mind and not get sidetracked on something material like what Satan offered Christ. We have to make sure that we put love first just like Jesus did.

And, believe me, putting love first isn't always easy. Jim and I know that. We have had some real bad hurts in the ministry, but God has always told us to forgive and not to judge.

When I think of how much Jesus loved us, I just cry sometimes. He stands up to Satan and goes on to carry out His Father's will. He wants to tell the world the "Good News" that God loves them, and what happens? John 1:11 says, "He came unto his own, and his own received him not." He was rejected. Jesus was rejected!

The fear of rejection is one of the biggest fears Satan tries to put on the Christian today. God created people for fellowship, and when we are rejected, it goes to the very core of our created being. Jim and I know what rejection means. We live with it daily. People we are trying to love turn on us or misunderstand us. And, boy, that hurts. At times it feels like we don't have a friend in the world.

What, Tammy, you mean you get rejected, too? A

big name like you who's on national television? Yup. Satan puffs me up to make me think I'm somebody, and then he bursts the bubble by making me feel rejected so that I feel like a nobody. Satan always is playing his tricks on us. The more we stay occupied on who we think we are and how important we are, the greater chance Satan has to torment us and make us try to defend ourselves and our ministry.

If I could get that roaring lion, Satan, I think I'd club him over the head sometimes. He makes me so mad.

Jesus, when rejected, kept loving. Oh, to be like our precious Jesus. He got hurt. The religious leaders of His day scoffed and laughed at him. Do you think that that didn't hurt? They tried to stone Him and even plotted His death. But did Jesus give up? No. He knew that the end of everything would be His victory. He saw that God's love would triumph.

Christ came to Jerusalem, Luke 19:41-42 records, "And when he was come near, he beheld the city, and wept over it, saying, If thou hadst known, even thou, at least in this thy day, the things which belong unto thy peace!" Jesus loved His people so much. He wept over them because of His great love. He came to bring them peace. But they rejected the Prince of Peace. That hurt so deeply.

I think all of us have experienced rejection at one time or another while we were simply trying to love. I know many people who have been so hurt in the church that they're afraid to get up and try to love again.

Satan would just love to keep us afraid to expose ourselves to others for fear of being hurt. He wants to keep us separated from each other and feeling all alone. Christ overcame the rejection and loved to the end. Christ, in John 15:12-13, says, **"This is my commandment, That ye love one another, as I have loved you. Greater love hath no man than this, that a man lay down his life for his friends."**

And our Jesus did just that; He laid down His life for us. He took on rejection so that we would not have to live with it. He took on our loneliness and sorrows so that we would be able to have fellowship and joy. He loved us at all costs!!

At times, we Christians don't realize how much Christ did for us. He came to heal the separation that we had. That old lion, Satan, tries to tell us something else, though. Christ defeated Satan's power through His death and resurrection. So now what can Satan do? Why, he can try to keep the body of Christ separated. Satan tries to keep Christians apart so that Christ can't return for His Church, "not having spot, or wrinkle, or any such thing," as Ephesians 5:27 says.

When we live in fear of rejection, we are falling right into Satan's trap. We have to run to the roar in that fear. I think one of the greatest things PTL Club is doing is making us Christians realize how we are all together as servants of Christ. One of our mottos for the abbreviation, PTL, is "People That Love." All of us have to unite and then love the world to Jesus.

In America today people live in such fear. There are so many of us, and things are moving so fast that we get lost in the shuffle. People feel that no one loves them. They feel rejected. We Christians have to reach out to these people and love them just as Jesus would.

If the body of Christ is going to reach out in love, then we better be able to walk in love. 1 Peter 4:8 tells us, **"And above all things have fervent charity (love) among yourselves."** We have got to love each other, and continue to love each other, and continue to love each other . . . no matter what. We can't listen to Satan's roaring about rejection.

A good example of someone in the Bible who had to overcome fear of rejection was Barnabas. This tender man sold his land and laid it at the apostles' feet to further the gospel and minister to poor saints. They named him the Son of Consolation; he must have been some man.

Can you imagine what his unsaved relatives must have said about him when he sold his land? Crazy, a fool, stupid, unwise. . . . He must have felt their rejection all right. They probably criticized him in the temple to let other Jews know that they didn't agree with his ridiculous conversion.

Barnabas held up, though, and grew in the faith. He had to grow because a big test was coming his way, a test that if passed would result in the conversion of thousands (even millions) of souls into God's kingdom. Of course, Barnabas didn't know this at the time, just as we often don't know the results of the tests we are going through.

The story is recorded in Acts 9. Barnabas was the one who was going to have to love the biggest enemy of the church and then convince the rest of the church to do the same. Imagine the fear that Satan must have tried to place in Barnabas' heart when Barnabas had to meet the notorious Saul of Tarsus.

Here's the man that watched the crowd stone Stephen, and now Barnabas was going to accept him as a brother in Christ. And, get this, not only did Barnabas take Saul in, but he talked to the rest of the church about doing the same.

Here's the account from Acts 9:26-27: "And when Saul was come to Jerusalem, he assayed to join himself to the disciples: but they were all afraid of him, and believed not that he was a disciple. But Barnabas took him, and brought him to the apostles, and declared unto them how he (Saul) had seen the Lord in the way, and that He had spoken to him, and how he had preached boldly at Damascus in the name of Jesus."

Barnabas was putting his reputation on the line. He was opening himself up to rejection by the church. After all, they were afraid of Saul already. What could Barnabas say to change their minds? Can't you just hear Satan whispering fearful thoughts into Barnabas' mind. "Your relatives have rejected you, and now the church is going to reject you. You better watch out. Don't blow it. They like you now, but if you side with Saul, the church will throw you to the wolves. Maybe the church is right; maybe Saul is tricking everyone so that he can find and kill all the Christians."

But the Son of Consolation would not listen to Satan's thoughts. He acted spiritually, and the great apostle Paul was accepted into the fellowship to become one of the fathers of the church. And all because a man overcame fear of rejection and loved Saul at any cost.

The story doesn't end here, either. Paul and Barnabas travelled all over, winning the lost to Christ and grounding Christians in the faith. Acts 14 records how Paul and Barnabas did such wonders that the people thought they were gods. At the city of Lystra they even called Barnabas, Jupiter. Imagine that. They thought Barnabas was their highest god! Things like that might go to the head of a lesser person, but Paul and Barnabas were humble servants of the Lord. They "rent" their clothes and preached to the people about the one true living God. Shortly after, Paul and

Barnabas were rejected; and Paul, actually stoned.

Barnabas had another major test to go through yet. Having passed all the other rejection tests, still one more test awaited him. And this test might have been the hardest of all because it involved the one he loved most in the Lord, the Apostle Paul. Let me recite the incident from Acts 15:36-41.

And some days after, Paul said unto Barnabas, Let us go again and visit our brethren in every city where we have preached the word of the Lord, and see how they do.

And Barnabas determined to take with them John, whose surname was Mark.

But Paul thought not good to take him with them, who departed from them from Pamphylia, and went not with them to the work.

And the contention was so sharp between them, that they departed asunder one from the other: and so Barnabas took Mark, and sailed unto Cyprus;

And Paul chose Silas, and departed, being recommended by the brethren unto the grace of God.

And he went through Syria and Cilicia, confirming the churches.

Can you imagine what was going on in Barnabas' mind. Here the man for whom he had risked his reputation, the man he had loved and had travelled with, the man he had probably shared more things with than anyone else, was at odds with him. Can't you hear the old lion roaring in Barnabas' ear, "Look at this love business. Christian love is all a pack of lies. You would've been better off if you never helped him. I told you Paul was no good. Paul's just out for his own glory. Now, how does it feel to be rejected? You give yourself for someone, and they stab you in the back."

The old devil must have been working overtime trying to split these men up and make them hate each other. And I asked myself, "Why would God allow this disagreement to be in the Bible?"

But let's look at the passage more closely. The Word doesn't say that these men stopped loving each other. It doesn't indicate that they resorted to fleshly tactics of name calling and accusing. Instead, the contention centered around the Lord's will in a particular matter.

Barnabas, who had befriended Paul when no one else would, now was befriending Mark, who had deserted Paul and Barnabas on an earlier occasion. Barnabas hadn't changed; he was still putting his neck on the line for others. And Paul hadn't changed; he was going to win the lost for Christ in the most powerful way he could.

Barnabas and Paul had come to a crossroads. God wanted their ministries to continue being perfected. But for this to happen the men would have to split up. If Paul and Barnabas had not loved each other so much, there probably would not even have been a contention. They would just have separated. But God was calling both of them into the next step in His will. Praise God. They were contending over God's will, not over personal goals.

Sometimes when God takes us to the next step in our lives, we become frustrated and confused and maybe even mad. God had it all under control. He knew that they would separate to increase the missionary ventures. He knew that they would depart as loving brothers in Christ who after the contention would see how God's hand was in the whole ordeal.

Satan could have had a victory celebration. He could have ended Paul's ministry and Barnabas' ministry. He could have destroyed them if they had listened to his roaring. "You don't love each other. You're being rejected. Jesus doesn't really love you." But Satan lost another battle. Barnabas and Paul, those dear saints in Christ, stayed spiritual. They didn't allow their fleshly nature to get in the way. They realized that God's will was most important. Christ's ministry was actually expanded rather than diminished.

And, people, we have to stay spiritual, too. We can't allow ourselves to resort to battles in the flesh. We have to love and take the risk of being rejected. We have to love and trust our Jesus to be faithful to His Word.

Chapter 8

RUNNING TO THE ROAR

After all these chapters about overcoming fears, I think it's about time I go into more detail of how I have to keep running to the roar in one of my greatest fears—fear of flying.

Shortly after Jim and I returned from Florida after the threats on our lives had been lifted, we decided we needed a vacation. Jim had been around the world several months before and had enjoyed Paris. So he thought it would be so nice for me to go back to my roots. You see, I am French.

I was a little leery. I said, "Lord, what am I going to do this first plane trip?

He said, "Well, Tammy, the first thing you have to do is to get on the airplane."

So I did. I went and faced the roar of that old jet engine that used to terrify me.

Just going to an airport would make me sick to my stomach. I mean, just going to an airport to see friends off, or going to an airport to see friends in, or just simply *going* to an airport. Just seeing an airplane go over put fear in my body so bad that I would look up and say, "Thank God I'm not up there."

But now I was so calm that I got on that plane and was able to take that trip . . . and enjoy it. God didn't ask me to endure it. He could have let me just endure the trip. But he caused me to enjoy it so much that, given a pillow, I went to sleep.

I don't even sleep in a car. I am a very light sleeper. I don't sleep anywhere. But, given a pillow in that airplane, I put my head over and went to sleep.

This sounds like I licked the fear real easy, right? Well, I came to find out it wasn't as easy as I thought.

After we came back from Paris, I had had my big victory. I had flown and I was excited and I had enjoyed it. I was really looking forward to more trips. And it just so happened that this year we had a lot of trips planned for PTL.

Our next trip was going to be to New York for one of the big crusades where Jim had been asked to minister. Two days before we were to leave on that flight, the big Chicago crash occurred, and hundreds of people were killed. My faith absolutely slipped down to half, and I said, "Ohhhhhhhh, God. What am I going to do now?"

All my faith just went zilch; I thought, "Here this great victory that I have won is gone." I had stood up in front of the people at PTL and told them the lion's story, and now what are they going to think? I'm not going to be able to get on this plane and fly to New York.

God spoke to me again and said, "Hey, the lion's story still works! You confess to the people one more time."

So we were standing in the television audience, and I said, "Well, we are getting ready to go to New York. You know what, people? I'm scared. The big Chicago crash kinda cut my faith down to half. I'm really nervous about it. So I'm going to run toward the roar of that lion again. I'm going to run right toward it, and I'm going to get on that plane and go."

After I confessed it, I knew that I would do it. So I went out to the airport and faced the roar of that jet engine again and got on and enjoyed that flight, and my faith was on again.

I believed God, but I also started listening to other things in my mind. I thought I could help God help me overcome my fear of flying.

I called the doctor and asked, "Doctor, could you prescribe something for me that would make it a little easier for me to fly?"

"Sure," he said, and he gave me a bottle of pills. I didn't know if they were tranquilizers or what. I had never taken anything like that before. He told me I should take one just before I got on the plane, and if I felt like it, I could take another one in four hours. I took one the minute I got them and another one three hours later as I was getting on the plane. Would you believe I was semi-stoned for two days.

I really got used to taking the "run to the roar pill." I knew taking these pills was a copout and not really totally running to the roar. And to make matters worse those close to me could tell I was taking them.

I prided myself that I was down to a half of one, but that still wasn't the freedom that I wanted or needed! I had to be totally free to fly on my own.

It is wonderful how God gives us close and real friends. Linda Wilson and Debbie Kartsonakis both asked me, "Tammy, when are you going to fly without the pills?" They said they could tell the moment I got off the plane if I had taken anything. Linda, who is also my secretary, declared up and down I was moving only at half speed when I had taken one of "the pills."

Debbie told me that I had a starry-eyed, glassy look that really made me look "spacey."

The Lord spoke to me and said, "Tammy, that isn't the way a child of Mine should look. Don't you think it is time that you totally trust Me?"

"Oh, yes Lord. Yes Lord. I want to be totally honest. Not only with you but with everyone who knows me and watches me on the PTL Club."

I decided right then and there that I had taken my very last pill!! I knew I could not write this book unless I was totally honest. I felt like taking the pills to fly was not being totally honest, and they were nothing but a crutch. The only time I ever took them was when I flew.

I was in Memphis finishing my latest record album and was booked on a flight from Memphis to Charlotte. I turned to Jim and said, "Honey, I'm not going to take a pill this time. I have it in my hand, but the Spirit of the Lord spoke to me and said, 'You don't need them!' So I thought, 'Well, Lord, O.K. You know; You know!'"

Then Satan really started fighting me and said, "Tammy, don't be such a fool. Don't you realize that the pills you are taking could be God's way for you to fly? Don't put yourself in such a spot. What if you get sick on the plane or you pass out or something like that—go ahead; it's O.K.; take a pill. God won't mind!"

For a moment I thought maybe I should. Who would know? After all, it really isn't sin. I knew then I had to run to the roar, and I did.

There was some fear as I boarded the plane, but as I took the seat, the fear left and faith swelled within me! God was with me and the lion had run!! Praise His Name!

God really helped me through that flight even though it was a very bumpy flight. It was a good flight for me, and I got off alive and talking fast like I usually do. With the help of God, I'm not going to ever have to take a pill again to fly!

God is our strength, and we do face fears every single day; and I'm not going to say I'll ever conquer my fears because with my type of personality, the kind of person I am, I probably never will conquer them totally, but I'm going to totally face them in faith and let faith overcome my fear! I lay claim right now on Philippians 4:13, "**I can do all things through Christ which strengtheneth me.**" The Bible says I am honoring God every time I get on an airplane.

Let's remember, every day is a new day to live in victory. We are told in Matthew 10:38 by Jesus Himself, "**He that taketh not his cross, and followeth after me, is not worthy of me.**" Friend, let's live and walk in faith as we run to the roar.

The more I have trusted the Lord, the more He has shown Himself to be the "All-Sufficient One." He has come in and met the need when I couldn't do it in myself. This third example will show that.

Debby and Dino and Jim and I went to General Council of the Assemblies of God. We were having fun in our motel room. I was singing opera and Dino was playing the piano. Debby started laughing so hard that she bent over double, and her mouth hit the piano and knocked out a quarter of her front tooth. We all felt terrible about it and knew she had to get it fixed immediately.

Wondering what to do, she remembered a dentist they had met in Iowa while in concert. He could fix teeth without capping, etc. We called him, and he said for Debby to come right away. She mentioned to him that I was coming, too, and had some teeth that had embarrassed me for years and could he look at them, too? He said he could, and we made our flight plans for eight o'clock the next morning.

Six the next morning came terribly early, and by the time we got to the airport, I was frazzled. We boarded the plane, and the plane took off. All of a sudden Debby's eyes got big and she said, "Tam, guess what; we are on a DC-10."

My heart went to my throat as I hoarsly said, "Debby, you could have talked all day long without saying that."

They had just put the planes back in the air after grounding them because of America's worst plane crash over the Memorial Day weekend. About 275 people had lost their lives when an engine broke off the DC-10 as it was taking off from Chicago's O'Hara International Airport. Now I had to fly back to the midwest on a DC-10.

Here I was in one, and there was nothing, absolutely nothing, I could do about it. With a terribly sick stomach I ran to the bathroom—not once but four times. Thoughts of that plane accident I had seen as a child jumped in and out of my mind. My mind was going 100 miles an hour, and the devil was really tormenting me. The weather was a little rough and the flight bumpy, and with every bump the devil nudged me again.

I could just see all those bodies scattered over the ground. People would be screaming and moaning. Those still alive would have legs or arms missing and be bloody all over. Maybe some of them would be trapped inside, and a fire would get them! The old devil was having a real ball, painting ugly thoughts that almost seemed to live in my mind.

I kept thinking about this book on conquering fear I was in the middle of writing, and I began to talk to the Lord. I said, "God, I just can't publish this book if I haven't conquered fear myself. What am I going to do?"

Then I got to thinking that it was teeth that had me in this predicament, and that if I wasn't so proud and wanted my own tiger teeth fixed, I wouldn't be on this plane. The more I thought, the worse the fear got and the sicker and more miserable I got.

Then Debby ordered breakfast, and the smell of eggs was more than I could take. I ran again for the bathroom. As the plane hit an air pocket, I was sure my time had come. Then I began to really pray and cry out to the Lord. "Lord, I can't let my book go to the press. It will be a lie. Help me; please help me."

Still this terrible fear . . . . Then all of sudden the peace of God that "passeth all understanding" came over me; my stomach settled down. He had heard my cry and came to my rescue. In His love He had replaced my fear with His peace.

You know, people, every single time in defeating the fear of anything, you become stronger. If you are afraid to go up an elevator for fear of the elevator dropping, you simply must face the fear head-on. We had to move out of a building that we were living in because I had gotten to where I was afraid of the elevator so bad. We were on the eighteenth floor, and I would lie there at night in the bed, and I would think there is only about two feet of wall between me and falling down seventeen stories. If I had known the lion's story, I would have faced that fear.

We must face it even if we have to face it daily. Don't run back to that little pack of demons that is going to destroy you. Fear could destroy your whole life and ministry. I was being robbed. Yes, sir, fear robs you of joy. Fear robs you of peace. Fear robs you of the things that are yours through Jesus. To me my life wasn't worth living. I had a terrible fear that we were going to lose PTL. I was afraid to fly. I was afraid of everything. I was afraid to go out of the house because of the threats on us. I was afraid to even go shopping for fear someone was going to grab me in the shopping center. I really got to the point where I thought life was not worth living anymore.

I knew Jesus was big enough to take care of me, and I really believed it, and I really felt that way. Now I had to walk in that faith. The Bible says, "It is appointed unto man once to die, but after this the judgment." We are all going to die at one time or another. So why sit we here and wait. Let's get up. We can be doing something while we are waiting to die.

A whole nation was fed because four leprous men faced the roar. They ran to the roar. They got up and said, "We are not going to lie here and die. It would be better to die," they said, "than to lie here like this. What's worse?" They went to the enemy camp and found that God had chased the fierce enemy all away. Instead of death, the men and the rest of Israel had food, clothing, and wealth. This story is told in 2 Kings 7:3-16.

I think there are times in life when it is better to die than to live a life so filled with fear and anguish that you can't ever be happy. I have given my life totally, 100 percent, to the Lord. If God wants me to go in an airplane, that's the way He will choose for me to go. I don't want to live if He isn't the head of my life anyway. It is important that we face that all the time. It's a daily battle. We are just human beings.

I think there are certain fears that could be

conquered forever. There are some fears that you have to face all the time. You have to keep running towards that roar, and there is such a victory and there is such a faith. The devil doesn't like victories. These things you are facing now; they are giving you victory. You have a new testimony—a new exciting thing that God has gotten you through!!

I have heard that "fear not" is mentioned 365 times in the Bible. FEAR NOT . . . for every day of the year. So God must know that every day we were going to have to face it.

Jesus didn't want to die. He faced the fear of that cross. He didn't want to die on that cross and have nails put through His hands. He didn't want a crown of thorns put on His head. Nobody would want to do that. He was a man just like us. But He faced the roar. He ran toward Satan and said, "You are not going to defeat me."

Remember when Jesus was up on the mountain, and he hadn't eaten for forty days? Satan came to Jesus and tempted Him. And Jesus said, "Get out of here, old boy (Tammy paraphrase). Man doesn't live by bread alone. You just get going the other way."

The Bible says, "Resist the devil, and he will flee from you." And we don't resist him by our own efforts. We use spiritual weapons because Satan is a spirit. God supplies the ammuniton. Christ is our conquering leader.

We just have to get our bodies to follow the spiritual direction. We Christians are spiritual, and we're on the winning side.

God said, "Resist him!" Resisting is just absolutely saying, "Hey, get out of here," and not giving in to him.

I think we as Christians have to do this literally.

We have to make it literal. When the devil comes upon us, all we have to say is, "Go away, Devil, in Jesus' name." We don't need to have a mad voice, but simply, according to the Word, say, "Go away, Devil. Go away, right now."

When the devil comes at us, we're not defenseless. Our loving Lord doesn't have us just stand up against Satan with no defense. He has us prepare ourselves.

Ephesians 6:10-11 says, **"Be strong in the Lord, and in the power of his might. Put on the whole armour of God, that ye may be able to stand against the wiles of the devil."**

Jesus knows (and so do we) that if we try to fight Satan with none of God's protection or defense, we will lose. So we have to put on the Lord's armor.

Ephesians 6:13-14 continues, **"Wherefore take unto you the whole armour of God, that ye may be able to withstand in the evil day, and having done all, to stand. Stand therefore, having your loins girt about with truth."**

I think God wants us to protect our sexual urges from Satan. In America and all over we are constantly bombarded with Satan's sexual traps. He gets housewives to watch soap operas on TV that show broken marriages and sexual fantasies. He gets teenagers to want to go to the shores of California where supposedly every girl and boy has a gorgeous body, and it is always "fun time" in a van.

Satan gets men to hide from admitting that they have strong sexual drives, and he makes them live in fear that they are not normal and that someone might find out that they do not have totally "pure" minds.

Girding our loins with truth means we go to the Word for answers (even sexual answers!) instead of going to the TV, the movies, or some magazine to "excite" us. God will protect us from Satan's sexual urges as we *live and walk* in truth, as we flood our minds with the Word.

Ephesians 6:14 continues that we should be **"having on the breastplate of righteousness."** this piece of armor protects the vital area of the heart. Before a person is saved, his heart "is deceitful above all things, and desperately wicked," according to Jeremiah 17:9. When we are saved, God cleanses our heart and protects us from Satan's sinful ways by allowing us to put on the breastplate of righteousness.

Ephesians says next to have our **"feet shod with the preparation of the gospel of peace."** Christ will guide our every step as we let Him. He will keep us away from turmoil to walk in peace if we allow His armor to do its work.

Verse 16 then says, **"Above all, taking the shield of faith, wherewith ye shall be able to quench all the fiery darts of the wicked."** That shield will protect us against every dart of fear that Satan can throw our way.

The final piece of armor is the **"helmet of salvation,"** according to verse 17. This will protect our mind and thoughts. Praise God.

Then with our armor in place, Christ equips us with **"the sword of the Spirit, which is the word of God."** We can attack Satan head-on with the sword. God didn't give us armor for our backside; He knew we'd never have to flee from Satan when we are in God's armor.

It was so cute, on my television show this little lady who was about ninety years old said she had problems with lapse of memory once in awhile. When she would have a lapse-of-memory problem, she would say, "Okay, devil, now you get out of here. You are trying to steal my thoughts. Get out of here." And instantly her thoughts would come back. Praise God, the Word works!

Chapter 9

FEAR OF DEATH

Overcoming the fear of flying made me realize that there are many situations in life that seem like a life-or-death situation. That DC-10 Debby and I were on could have crashed. We could have been in a fatal car accident on the way to the airport. Our motel could have burned down, trapping us inside. We could have eaten poisoned food. It seems that most everything in life could lead to our death.

If we listen to Satan, he will keep us in fear of death. We have to keep our eyes on Jesus who is the author of life, or we will end up doing nothing and going nowhere and speaking to no one. In other words, we end up not being human. Life itself is a calculated risk. Everything we do could bring disaster, but if we dwell on that, that will be disaster too.

We can choose life or death. Once we have chosen life (that is, accepted Christ into our hearts to run our lives), we have to turn off that old roar of Satan.

Christ took on death at Calvary so that Satan's scare tactics about death would be meaningless. Hebrews 2:14-15 explains Christ's experience on the Cross **"that through death He might destroy him that** had the power of death, that is, the devil; and deliver them who through fear of death were all their lifetime subject to bondage."

You see, we Christians don't have to fear death anymore. Jesus already conquered the old lion Satan who had death in his hands. Now all that lion can do is roar and fuss and fume. Christ also freed us who were in bondage to death that we might walk in eternal life right now and not worry about the old lion's lying noises. Jesus has so much more of life for us if we will only stop worrying about death.

Mr. Tom Hoogerland, a chaplain during the Viet Nam War, wrote to me when he found out I was doing this book to give an example of really running to the roar in a life-or-death situation:

When our young soldiers were being trained for Viet Nam, they were taught how to react to an ambush. They were taught to move toward the firing. For example, if some soldiers were moving along a trail and someone began shooting at them from their right, they were to move toward the firing.

The reason behind this training is this: those who had set up the ambush would have set mines and bobby traps along the left side of the trail. The normal reaction to being fired upon would be to take cover and to move away from the apparent danger. Experience taught that the best course of action was to go against the normal inclination. The greatest danger was in moving away rather than toward the "roar," just like you are saying.

If the army knows this tactic, it's about time we Christians apply it to our spiritual warfare as well.

The story of Esther in the Old Testament is a

good example of someone who had to face life-or-death situations and run to the roar.

Her whole life had been lived in fear. The terror of the captivity, the tragic death of both her parents, and now this. Her Uncle Mordecai wanted her to go join the royal harem. The ignominy of it! To be used, perhaps only once, and discarded for life. Condemned to serve forever as a royal reject.

Oh yes, she knew that some of the maidens in the kingdom would give their best veil for such an opportunity, but not Esther. She wanted a husband, not a king; a home, not a palace; babies, not royal heirs. She longed for a family to replace the one that had been taken from her, and the fear that none of this might ever be hers almost suffocated her.

As if all this were not enough, her uncle cautioned her to keep her nationality a secret, for it was despised. So she must also live with the fear of bigotry and exposure. Oh, Jehovah, was there never to be an end to her fears?

And then in a matter of days it was over. She was safe. She had been crowned the Queen of Persia. No one could threaten her without risking the king's wrath. No one could slight or ignore her ever again. She was safe.

Months went by. Happy, exciting, glorious days became memories as she learned to preside over her royal duties. But suddenly, due to a treacherous betrayal, she must risk it all, even her very life. She must approach her husband the king, unbidden, and this could invoke the death penalty. Then she must deliberately reveal her background and ask for mercy for herself and her people. How this royal orphan must have trembled as she braced herself to do what she must.

It was at this point that she said, "Who knows but whether I have come to the kingdom for such a time as this." What Esther was saying was, "Perhaps I was born to face this fear for either the salvation or destruction of both myself and others."

So she faced her fear. The king gave mercy, her people were saved, and her enemies destroyed.

God help us to remember that we are joint-heirs with Christ, not just royal orphans, when it is time to face our fears.

Esther sacrificed everything she had to protect her people. And the result? She found favor in the kings's eyes, Haman—the Jew's enemy—was executed, and the Jews all won favor and gained rule over those who were ruling them. Wow! That's just like God to turn fear of death into victory.

Another of God's servents, Samuel, ran the risk of death in his obedience to God in 1 Samuel 15 and 16. Saul had "blown it;" his disobedience to God finally cost him his position as king. When God told the prophet Samuel about Saul, Samuel grieved. He had to break the news to King Saul. And after he told Saul, God directed him to anoint someone else as king. Poor Samuel continued to grieve for Saul (and maybe for himself as well).

God spoke to Samuel. "How long will you go on grieving over Saul? I have rejected him as king of Israel." Then He commanded Samuel to go to Jesse and anoint one of his sons to be king.

Samuel quickly counted the cost. "How can I do that?" he asked. "If Saul hears about it, he will kill me!"

Fear. Fear of Saul's anger—fear of dying. Samuel knew Saul's temper. His fear was reasonable. Instead of rebelling, though, he took his fears to God. "How can I do that?'' God did not rebuke him for his fear. He did not demand unquestioning obedience. All He asked was a willing heart.

God gave Samuel a cover—a means by which he could go to Jesse without arousing the suspicions of Saul. "Take a calf with you and say that you are there to offer a sacrifice to the Lord. Invite Jesse to the sacrifice, and I will tell you what to do.''

Samuel had seen the results of disobedience in Saul's life. Yet it wasn't fear of God which motivated his obedience. Samuel was able to obey, to over-ride his fears, because he *trusted* God. God had met him at his point of need. While the risks still remained, so did God. His hand was upon the work that Samuel was called to do.

We have a reasonable God. He never asks us to do anything that He does not equip us to do.

Samuel put his trust in the Lord and obeyed and overcame the fears. Oh, how our Lord desires for us to walk in obedience to Him. As we obey in love, our fears are removed. We start seeing how faithful God is to take care of our every need. Why should we fear death or peril when we are in love with Jesus? Jesus said in John 10:10, **"I am come that they might have life, and that they might have it more abundantly."** Fear takes our eyes off that abundant life, but the more we are in love with Jesus, the more we see that we do have abundant life.

In my years in the ministry I've seen so many people who haven't discovered how abundant life can be in Jesus. I've seen Christians play spiritual games rather than walk in obedience to the Lord. And their outcome is so predictable. Fear comes into their lives. Nothing seems to go right. They may continue to go to church and even be active in church work, but their heart is on longer in accord with Jesus' will. Then it is that fear becomes real. Trouble and fear; fear and trouble. Nothing seems to go right.

It's worse than my fear of flying was. I'm not on an airplane twenty-four hours a day. But people out of fellowship with God carry their fear with them all the time. I mean 1440 minutes a day. God describes how people out of fellowship with Him will act in Deuteronomy 28: 65-67:

But the LORD shall give thee there a trembling heart, and failing of eyes, and sorrow of mind: And thy life shall hang in doubt before thee; and thou shalt fear day and night, and thou shalt have none assurance of thy life: In the morning thou shalt say, Would God it were even! and at even thou shalt say, Would God it were morning! for the fear of thine heart wherewith thou shalt fear, and for the sight of thine eyes which thou shalt see.

But listen what God promises those who walk in obedience to Him:

And it shall come to pass, if thou shalt hearken diligently unto the voice of the LORD thy God, to observe and to do all his commandments which I command thee this day, that the LORD thy God will set thee on high above all nations of the earth:

And all these blessings shall come on thee, and overtake thee, if thou shalt hearken unto the voice of the LORD thy God.

Blessed shalt thou be in the city, and blessed shalt thou be in the field.

Blessed shall be the fruit of thy body, and the fruit of thy ground, and the fruit of thy cattle, the increase of thy kind, and the flocks of thy sheep.

Blessed shall be thy basket and thy store.

Blessed shalt thou be when thou comest in, and blessed shalt thou be when thou goest out.

The LORD shall cause thine enemies that rise up against thee to be smitten before thy face: they shall come out against thee one way, and flee before thee seven ways.

The LORD shall command the blessing upon thee in thy storehouses, and in all that thou settest thine hand unto; and he shall bless thee in the land which the LORD thy God giveth thee.

The LORD shall establish thee a holy people unto himself, as he hath sworn unto thee, if thou shalt keep the commandments of the LORD thy God, and walk in his ways. And all the people of the earth shall see that thou art called by the name of the LORD: and they shall be afraid of thee.

And the LORD shall make thee plenteous in goods, in the fruit of thy body, and in the fruit of thy cattle, and in the fruit of thy ground, in the land which the LORD sware unto thy fathers to give thee. The LORD shall open unto thee his good treasure, the heaven to give the rain unto thy land in his season, and to bless all the work of thine hand: and thou shalt lend unto many nations, and thou shall not borrow.

And the LORD shall make thee the head, and not the tail; and thou shalt be above only, and thou shalt not be beneath; if that thou hearken unto the commandments of the LORD thy God, which I command thee this day, to observe and to do them:

And thou shalt not go aside from any of the words which I command thee this day, to the right hand, or to the left, to go after other gods to serve them (Deut. 28:1-14).

Talk about powerful promises. It makes me just weep and cry sometimes to think how good God is to those who love Him. It seems that when I take one step toward Him, He takes about a hundred steps toward me. He is so willing to meet us and love us if we only let Him. He takes us through the trials, and sometmes I think he even puts earplugs in our ears so that we don't hear Satan's roars about death or trouble. The closer we are to Jesus, the more we realize that we are with the best lion tamer of all times.

If Satan can't convince us we are going to die, he tries a different tactic. He takes us as far astray as we will let him. If he can't scare us with death, he will scare us with sickness. I don't know how many times I've worried about catching the latest flu bug or whatever is going around. I say, "Jesus, I can't get sick now. I've got too much work to do. I've got to work on this record and not get behind schedule. I've got to host PTL; I've got to . . . ; I've got to . . . "

Before I know it, I'm starting to worry so much that I get that run-down feeling. And that opens the door for the old flu bug or whatever. Satan has won another victory. I know some people who are sick almost all the time. It seems like they look for something to catch. They walk in sickness because Satan has convied them they can't walk in health. Some of them are hypochondriacs. Satan has made them believe the lie that getting sympathy or worrying about their physical health is more important than Christ's abundant life.

I know of one man who would never go to a doctor because he was afraid of what the doctor might say. His father and his brother had both died of heart attacks, and high blood pressure ran in the family. So for eighteen years he didn't go to the doctor; even when he had pains, he stayed away from the doctor. The outcome was that very recently he had a heart attack and died instantly.

Imagine that! Satan scares us into fearing about our health and tries to make us do things that lead us to death. Christian, do what's right. Don't believe Satan's lies in your mind. He'll keep you in constant fear. Sometimes God's healing comes through doctors.

Listen, Christian, we don't have all the answers about health and God's will. But we do have the precious Holy Spirit who, according to John 16:13, will guide us into all truth. Why, I wonder how many doctors have come to know Christ because they had some sick, but godly, patients. We don't always know why we are sick. Jim and I know, though, that **"all things work together for good to them that love God, to them who are the called according to his purpose,"** as Romans 8:28 says.

We have to trust God in the circumstances and keep our eyes on Him and not on our problems. Satan tells us all sorts of lies, and if we keep our minds open to his lies, he will lead us to disaster. Our minds are the battleground where Satan often can win a victory if we don't recognize his tactics. We must balance our thoughts with prayer, the Word of God, and mature Christian counsel.

Satan whispers lies to us all the time about death or sickiness. If we listen to him, he will paralyze us so that we can't live full lives. We have to be so careful, too, what we say to our children. If we preach fear, they will live in fear.

Let me give you an example that I heard from a friend. She was being taught in church when she was younger that it was a privilege to die for the Lord. During the discussion the teacher told the class the story of how this one Christian had been persecuted. The teacher said that this Christian martyr had had her stomach cut open and a rat placed inside to eat her to death. The teacher also said that other Christians had had their heads cut off because they would not deny Christ; some burned at the stake.

The children in the class were then asked to raise their hands if they would be willing to die for Christ. Well, the whole class, including the woman who related this story to me, raised their hands. But, inside, fear gripped her heart.

This woman said that from that time on she had been afraid of being persecuted for Christ. That was over thirty years ago and that horrible fear remained for years and years.

It's just like when I was growing up and religious leaders asked us Christian kids if we would stay true to Jesus even if the Communists took over. Of course we would, but deep down we started fearing the Communists.

We don't know the specific circumstances that are ahead for us, but I know that Jesus can take us through anything. Christ promised us in Matthew 10:19-20 that we should not even worry so much as what to say in time of great turmoil because "the Spirit of your Father" will even give us words.

And, after all, if we're Christians, we have already died to the world and are alive unto Christ. Christ doesn't want us to prove that we love Him by having to be a martyr some day. I can't find that in the Bible anywhere. He doesn't want our acts; He wants us. He wants us to live for Him and in Him right now. We can't worry about tomorrow. Our tomorrows are in our loving Christ's hands. We are only as spiritual as we are right now. Satan is the one who wants us to worry about our futures.

If you want your kids to be loving Christians, then teach them love. If you want your kids to be fearing Christians, then teach them fear. Parents' lives are examples that their kids will follow.

I saw Jim and Tammy and even their little children run to the roar.

Jim, Tammy, and I had been out for dinner. We had been going over notes for this book, and Tammy wanted to go out for a little farewell party for me before I returned to Arkansas.

We had left Susie and Jamie with the sitter. During the meal Jim and Tammy both said they wished the children were with us.

The day for me had been somewhat exciting because that morning there had been a bomb threat at the PTL Club studios. Very quietly after the show we had all been asked to leave the building.

"Jim," I asked, "aren't you afraid of these constant threats?"

"Sometimes, Cliff, but we have really given them over to the Lord. If we would close up every time something like this happened, we'd never get anything done," was his reply.

On the way back to the Bakker house after dinner, a strange and foreboding feeling came over me. "Lord, what's wrong?" I asked.

When we pulled in the drive, I said, "Look at all the cars? I wonder what's going on."

We were met by Phil Eggert, Jim's assistant, who said, "Don't worry. Everything is under control. Barbara has taken the children to her house, and they are O.K.

"*Jim, we had another bomb threat. We were told your house was wired to blow up at 1:00 A.M. The police and firemen have just left, and they could not find a thing.*

"*To play it safe we made reservations for you at a motel and are prepared to take you there right now.*"

By now fear had gripped my heart. I was all for going, and the sooner the better!

Just then Tammy stepped forward and said, "Oh no we don't. We are going to stay right here. Phil, call and have Barbara bring the children back. God is with us, and we are not going to run!"

Phil looked at Jim, and Jim nodded in agreement.

Tammy continued, "If we run now, we will never stop. That caller is getting his kicks out of our fear, and this is it. We're staying! If Cliff and I are going to do this book, then we have got to stay and show everyone that our strength is in the Lord."

Soon the children were back, and we popped popcorn and fellowshipped in Jesus.

Needless to say, the bomb didn't go off. But you should have heard my heart ticking around one A.M.! By seven the next morning I, too, was able to run to the roar.

Chapter 10

"Thy Word Have I Hid . . .

. . . in my heart that I might not sin against thee"
(Ps. 119:11).

We have already, I trust, established that fear is
sin and is not pleasing to God! Therefore, if we are to
overcome fear, we must have Scriptures readily
available to combat the darts of fear that Satan will
constantly be throwing at us, God's children.

The following verses have really meant a lot to me
and have been a fortress in helping me overcome my
fears. I believe if you will memorize these and hide
them in your heart, you also will experience the
victory that Jesus wants you to have.

IN PRAISE FEAR LEAVES

"What time I am afraid, I will trust in thee. In God I will praise his word, in God I have put my trust; I will not fear what flesh can do unto me" (Ps. 56:3-4).

"In God have I put my trust: I will not be afraid what man can do unto me" (Ps. 56:11).

In the midst of praise and worship fear must leave. Strange isn't it, when we should be full of praise, we keep silent. I have a new song I enjoy singing so much because it is a song of praise. The name of it is, "We're Blessed." As a matter of fact, I've named my new record album after that song. Whenever I sing it, God always moves in power, and there is never fear present!

I never fail to feel the presence of the Lord when I sing this song. It seems that when we praise the Lord, fear leaves! Fear and praise can't dwell in the same temple.

FEAR OF THE UNKNOWN

"He that dwelleth in the secret place of the most High shall abide under the shadow of the Almighty. I will say of the lord, He is my refuge and my fortress: my God; in him will I trust.

"Surely he shall deliver thee from the snare of the fowler, and from the noisome pestilence. He shall cover thee with his feathers, and under his wings shalt thou trust: his truth shall be thy shield and buckler.

"Thou shalt not be afraid for the terror by night; nor for the arrow that flieth by day; nor for the pestilence that walketh in darkness; nor for the destruction that wasteth at noonday.

"A thousand shall fall at thy side, and ten thousand at thy right hand; but it shall not come nigh thee" (Ps. 91:1-7).

There certainly is nothing I could add to these verses except to cry and thank Jesus that He is truly my refuge and fortress, and He keeps me from all harm!

FEAR OF BAD NEWS

"Praise ye the Lord. Blessed is the man that feareth the Lord, that delighteth greatly in his commandments .... He shall not be afraid of evil tidings: his heart is fixed, trusting in the Lord"
(Ps. 112:1, 7).

At two in the morning the telephone rings! What is the result—fear strikes. Our first thought is, "What's wrong; who has died?" Or when we get a registered letter or telegram, fear wells up in our heart.

The above verse says that we delight in His commandments, we need not even be afraid of evil tidings.

FEAR OF DEATH

"Yea, though I walk through the valley of the shadow of death, I will fear no evil: for thou art with me; thy rod and thy staff they comfort me" (Ps. 23:4).

What's heaven like? Is there really life after death? How am I going to die? Will I suffer? Will I be able to praise God in death? Satan wants us to be fearful over death—but God is there!

As the shepherd cares for the little sheep, and the mother for her nursing child; so God cares and comforts His own.

Remember, to be absent from the body is to be present with the Lord!

FEAR OF DAMNATION

"For as many as are led by the Spirit of God, they are the sons of God.

"For ye have not received the spirit of bondage again to fear; but ye have received the spirit of adoption, whereby we cry, Abba, Father.

"The Spirit itself beareth witness with our spirit, that we are the children of God" (Rom. 8:14-16).

"Behold, God is my salvation; I will trust, and not be afraid: for the LORD JEHOVAH is my strength and my song; he also is become my salvation" (Isa. 12:2).

One of the meanest tricks of Satan is to try to convince Christians that they really aren't saved or have lost their salvation or the Bible is a bunch of lies. What a place of torment if we buy that. God is my Daddy and His Spirit tells me so every day.

He loves and cares for me far more than I am capable of loving my own Tammy Sue and Jamie.

To think that Jesus loves us more than we could ever love our children, our mate, or our parents— what a wonderful love God has for us.

FEAR OF SATAN

"The Lord is my light and my salvation; whom shall I fear? The Lord is the strength of my life; of whom shall I be afraid?" (Ps. 27:1).

There are two forces in the world—God and Satan. We are in the middle. When we speak fear, doubt, and negativism, Satan comes toward us and does his own thing. He has an invitation to work. When we speak faith and trust, God comes toward us. We give Him a chance to work.

So we have a choice. Satan will go as far in our lives as we allow him to go and so will God. It is up to us!

FEAR OF BEING
IN THE TIMID MINORITY

"Be not afraid nor dismayed by reason of the great multitude; for the battle is not yours, but God's" (2 Chron. 20:15).

During my school years and many times since, waves of being an outsider sometimes hit me. You know what I mean. You're the only Christian in the family or in the school or where you work. Satan wants to make us feel small and not with it!!

At times like that I have to remember whose family I belong to. My family is the mightiest in the universe, and my Father has all power. I'm not an outsider; I'm on the inside. Satan's the one who's on the outside.

I'M NOBODY AND
FORGOTTEN BY GOD

"Are not five sparrows sold for two farthings, and not one of them is forgotten before God?

"But even the very hairs of your head are all numbered. Fear not therefore: ye are of more value than many sparrows" (Luke 12:6-7).

Just think people! God cares for the sparrow—so what are we worried about? He loves me so much that He knows the very number of hairs on my head—even if I'm wearing a wig! Ha. Ha. So let's declare before all that we are somebody. We are children of Almighty God.

FEAR OF MAN

*"The fear of man bringeth a snare: but whoso putteth his trust in the L*ORD *shall be safe"* (Pro. 29:25).

"Let your conversation be without covetousness; and be content with such things as ye have: for he hath said, I will never leave thee, nor forsake thee.

*"So that we may boldly say, The L*ORD *is my helper, and I will not fear what man shall do unto me"* (Heb. 13:5-6).

*"I, even I, am he that comforteth you: who art thou, that thou shouldest be afraid of a man that shall die, and of the son of man which shall be made as grass; and forgettest the L*ORD *thy maker, that hath stretched forth the heavens, and laid the foundations of the earth; and has feared continually every day because of the fury of the oppressor?"* (Isa. 51:12-13).

"Hearken unto me, ye that know righteousness, the people in whose heart is my law; fear ye not the reproach of men, neither be ye afraid of their revilings" (Isa. 51:7).

"What time I am afraid, I will trust in thee.

"In God I will praise his word, in God I have put my trust; I will not fear what flesh can do unto me" (Ps. 56:3-4).

"The LORD is my light and my salvation; whom shall I fear? the LORD is the strength of my life; of whom shall I be afraid?" (Ps. 27:1).

"Though an host should encamp against me, my heart shall not fear: though war should rise against me, in this will I be confident" (Ps. 27:3).

No comment!

FEAR OF LOVE COMMITMENT

"Herein is our love made perfect, that we may have boldness in the day of judgment: because as he is, so are we in this world.

"There is no fear in love; but perfect love casteth out fear: because fear hath torment. He that feareth is not made perfect in love" (1 John 4:17-18).

The scripture tells us to love, love, love. But because of all the strange stories we hear, it seems to be a fearful part of life! But when we really have faith in God, our love is made perfect, and we can jump right in; for we know that God is also there to keep that love pure, holy, and undefiled.

ANXIETY

"Peace I leave with you, my peace I give unto you: not as the world giveth, give I unto you. Let not your heart be troubled, neither let it be afraid" (John 14:27).

Today we live in a troubled world. The oil crisis is now upon us; inflation seems to be taking over. Our dollar is falling, the threat of war is upon us. But in the midst of all of this Jesus says, "My peace I give unto you." There is truly peace in the midst of the storm when we know Jesus.

FEAR THAT GOD
DOESN'T HEAR OUR PRAYER

"And, behold, an hand touched me, which set me upon my knees and upon the palms of my hands.

"And he said unto me, O Daniel, a man greatly beloved, understand the words that I speak unto thee, and stand upright: for unto thee am I now sent. And when he had spoken this word unto me, I stood trembling.

"Then said he unto me, Fear not, Daniel: for from the first day that thou didst set thine heart to understand, and to chasten thyself before thy God, thy words were heard and I am come for thy words"(Dan. 10:10-12).

"I will bless the LORD at all times: his praise shall continually be in my mouth.

"My soul shall make her boast in the LORD: the humble shall hear thereof, and be glad.

"O magnify the LORD with me, and let us exalt his name together.

"I sought the LORD, and he heard me, and delivered me from all my fears" (Ps. 43:1-4).

It seems that so often God turns a deaf ear to our prayers. When this happens, it's a good idea to begin to praise the Lord anyhow. If there is any sin in your life, confess it so He indeed will hear you.

Sometimes it seems as though the heavens are brass, but that is the time to cry out to God in a loud voice in faith believing that He hears. If one verse of the Bible is false, it voids the whole Book.

I choose to believe God's Word is true and that every promise in the Book is mine. Therefore, I know He hears my prayers.

GOD WILL DEFEND US

"And Moses said unto the people, Fear ye not, stand still, and see the salvation of the LORD, which he will shew to you today: for the Egyptians whom ye have seen today, ye shall see them again no more for ever.

"The LORD shall fight for you, and ye shall hold your peace" (Exod. 14:13-14).

"Say to them that are of a fearful heart, Be strong, fear not: behold, your God will come with vengeance, even God with a recompence; he will come and save you" (Isa. 35:4).

Oftentimes I get so hurt by people who are jealous or just plain mean. And from all the letters I get, a lot of you are also hurt. Well, our first reaction is to lash out and try to hurt back. Words spoken in anger seem to do harm forever.

When I apply the Word to my hurt, God softens me and takes care of the other person. We need to stand still more often.

FEAR OF PEOPLE
DESTROYING OUR REPUTATION

"Fear thou not: for I am with thee: be not dismayed: for I am thy God: I will strengthen thee; yea, I will help thee; yea, I will uphold thee with the right hand of my righteousness.

"Behold, all they that were incensed against thee shall be ashamed and confounded: they shall be as nothing; and they that strive with thee shall perish.

"Thou shalt seek them, and shalt not find them, even them that contended with thee: they that war against thee shall be as nothing, and as a thing of nought" (Isa. 41:10-13).

Recently Jim had some men who wanted to destroy his reputation and were bold enough to even tell him so. But their plan didn't work, and as this scripture says, they were really sat upon by the Lord. We really need to be careful before we do anything against God's anointed!

Isn't it wonderful to be under His protection and know that you are His anointed.

RUN TO THE ROAR

"Ye shall not need to fight in this battle: set yourselves, stand ye still, and see the salvation of the LORD *with you, O Judah and Jerusalem: fear not, nor be dismayed; tomorrow go out against them: for the* LORD *will be with you.*

"And Jehoshaphat bowed his head with his face to the ground: and all Judah and the inhabitants of Jerusalem fell before the LORD, *worshipping the* LORD*"* (2 Chron. 20:17-18).

"Submit yourselves therefore to God. Resist the devil, and he will flee from you" (James 4:7).

Every day it seems like a new kind of fear creeps into our lives. The first time I was to host PTL all alone, I was so afraid I couldn't do it that I could hardly sleep. But praise the Lord, the battle is indeed His. I hosted the show and really felt God's presence.

Jim has the motto, "The Battle is the Lord's," all over PTL and it works!

HIS PROMISE OF JOY

"In that day it shall be said to Jerusalem, Fear thou not: and to Zion, Let not thine hands be slack.

"The LORD thy God in the midst of thee is mighty; he will save, he will rejoice over thee with joy; he will rest in his love, he will joy over thee with singing" (Zeph. 3:16-17).

As a mother it is interesting to look back after giving birth to my children. Yes, there is a slight rememberance of pain, but what I really remember is the joy—joy unspeakable as I saw the new life that came from within me!! Tears of joy, and it seemed like bushels of laughter with the sheer delight of birth. Don't all of you mothers agree?

The joy that God gives does not even depend on circumstances. Jesus loves to create joy within us because He loves us so.

FEAR OF FEAR ITSELF

"Be not afraid of sudden fear, neither of the desolation of the wicked, when it cometh. For the LORD *shall be thy confidence, and shall keep thy foot from being taken"* (Prov. 3:25-26).

"For God hath not given us the spirit of fear; but of power, and of love, and of a sound mind" (2 Tim. 1:7).

This one says it all!

I don't profess to have conquered fear completely. I don't think any of us ever will, me especially. But I daily face my fears.

If we daily run to the roar with faith in God, it will make our lives so much easier and worthwhile—happy and victorious.